W9-CFU-525

CO-AVX-781

LIBERALISM, SOCIALISM AND CHRISTIAN SOCIAL ORDER

LIBERALISM, SOCIALISM AND CHRISTIAN SOCIAL ORDER

BOOK 3
Private Property as a Social Institution

Heinrich Pesch

Translated by
Rupert J. Ederer

Mellen Studies in Economics
Volume 7

The Edwin Mellen Press
Lewiston•Queenston•Lampeter

HB
95
.P3813
2000
v.3

Library of Congress Cataloging-in-Publication Data

Pesch, Heinrich, 1854-1926.
   [Liberalismus, Sozialismus und christliche Gesellschaftsordnung. English]
   Liberalism, socialism, and Christian social order / Heinrich Pesch ; translated by Rupert
J. Ederer.
      p. cm. -- (Mellen Studies in economics ; v. 7)
   Contents: bk. 3 Private property as a social institution --
   ISBN 0-7734-7587-7 (v. 3)
   1. Free enterprise. 2. Liberalism. 3. Socialism. I. Title. II. Series.

HB95 .P3813   2001
320.5'1--dc21

                                 99-088233

This is volume 7 in the continuing series
Mellen Studies in Economics
Volume 7 ISBN 0-7587-7
MSEc Series ISBN 0-7734-7966-X

A CIP catalog record for this book is available from the British Library.

Copyright © 2001 Rupert J. Ederer

The Edwin Mellen Press
Box 450
Lewiston, New York
USA 14092-0450

The Edwin Mellen Press
Box 67
Queenston, Ontario
CANADA L0S 1L0

The Edwin Mellen Press, Ltd.
Lampeter, Ceredigion, Wales
UNITED KINGDOM SA48 8LT

Printed in the United States of America

This Work is Dedicated to My Daughter Mary
Whose Disinterest in Private Property Amid a Materialistic Culture is Most Refreshing.

Contents

Translator's Foreword

Private Property as a Social Institution is the third book in the Edwin Mellen series presenting the first English translation of the works on social philosophy and economics by Heinrich Pesch S. J. (1854-1926) It is a part of his two volume work *Liberalism, Socialism, and Christian Social Order*. These volumes are divided into five books including this one which appeared originally in 1900 as *Das Privateigenthum als sociale Institution*.

When Pesch set about writing his monumental five volume *Lehrbuch der Nationalökonomie* in 1905, he drew heavily on the elements of social philosophy which he had developed in this earlier work. Specifically the institution, private property, is included in the first volume of the *Lehrbuch* as one of the basic foundations of the social order. There we have the essence of how he understood private property as a vital institution that is encumbered with social responsibilities. Heinrich Pesch's own position is stated concisely in the first few paragraphs under the heading of the *Author's Introduction*. It follows the Aristotelian-Thomistic teaching on private property which, in turn, was adapted to the then modern context of society by Leo XIII in *Rerum Novarum* just nine years before Pesch published this book.

The author proceeds to analyze what were from that natural law perspective the flawed Enlightenment notions of how private property originated. These included the *contract* and *legal* theories, followed by the evolutionistic approach which was then readily adapted to modern socialism.

Pesch addressed general objections to the private property institution in the sixth chapter. Here he dispensed with a certain perennial confusion between a general indictment of the institution, private property, and a voluntary rejection of private ownership based on evangelical counsels of perfection. In support of such misunderstanding, references from Sacred Scripture and certain statements by early Church Fathers have been adduced. Thus, even socialists who otherwise have little regard for such sources have cited them in support of their own absolutist rejection of the institution itself.

What may come as a surprise to some readers is an entire chapter (sixth) devoted to the *Open Letter to His Holiness Pope Leo XIII* by the American social reformer Henry George (1839-1897). George's works were widely read also abroad, and certain German translations went through several editions. He came to be known especially for what was to be his obsessive preoccupation - *the single tax* on the appreciation in land value which, he concluded, would make all other taxes unnecessary. This fanciful and simplistic panacea was based on George's belief that land appreciates naturally without its owners contributing to such increase in value. He has followers still; and his preaching to Leo XIII, whose position Pesch defends, is an interesting and mostly overlooked part of George's endeavors.

As an antidote to what Heinrich Pesch regarded as flawed reasoning about private ownership, whether by George or by earlier socialistic and other opponents of the institution itself, the Jesuit scholar presented the standard Scholastic defense. This included what came to be known as three original titles to ownership (occupation, accretion, and labor), and two derivative ones (hereditary and contractual). Under the latter, we find what was substantially the basis for the distinctive interest and usury analysis included in the fifth volume of the *Lehrbuch* (1923) under income distribution.

The final chapter on the *Obligations and Limits on Private Property* is already very specific to Pesch's solidarist economics. It contains what sets that economic schema apart from the notion of private ownership which became essentially a part of liberal capitalism from it beginnings until now. Its absolute concept of private ownership can be called *classical* in a double sense by virtue of its being implicit in early classical economics, and because it reverts, as the Russian writer Nicholas Berdyaev indicated, to what prevailed in ancient Rome. For Heinrich Pesch, the right of private property is not absolute. Being a social institution - one that is exercised in society among other human beings with co-equal rights - it is conditioned by the rights of other individuals as well as by the common good of society. That is a consideration which impacts not only on such matters as the *right of eminent domain* and contract rights, but also on the needs of other members of society especially the less fortunate ones, as well as ecological concerns which were never a factor in the capitalistic order until very recently. Stated in summary and succinct form, the Peschian position as it emerges in this work is: while there is a natural right to private property, its use must always be social, i.e., socially responsible.

Translator's Foreword

My special thanks are owed to Dr. Peter Danner, friend and colleague since graduate school days at St. Louis University. He has encouraged me continuously in my effort to make Pesch's work known, and he graciously supplied the *Preface* for this volume. As always, I must express appreciation also to my son, Dr. Martin Ederer, for his careful proof-reading and editorial suggestions.

Preface

English-only Social Economists and other scholars concerned about economic morality are forever in debt to Dr. Ederer for the years he spent translating and bringing to press Heinrich Pesch's two major works, *Liberalism, Socialism, and Christian Social Order*, of which *Private Property as a Social Institution* is one part, and the monumental five volume *Lehrbuch der Nationalökonomie*. I know this has been a labor of love for decades — but a burden none the less and a cause now of great rejoicing that the Edwin Mellen Press has brought this effort to fruition. More than this, it is a way of honoring two scholars he — and I — hold in great esteem. Rev. Bernard W. Dempsey, S. J. and Prof. Franz H. Mueller.

But beyond paying a filial debt, Ederer has made available a valuable resource for economists and other social scientists who are concerned to blend economic principles into an holistic pattern of living — economic, civil, social and moral — called Solidarism. William R. Waters, for many years professor of economics at De Paul University and editor of the *Review of Social Economy,* has described Solidarism well:

As the theory [Solidarism] has progressed to date, it describes a socially just economy as one populated by persons (instead of rational utility maximizers) who make choices combining motives of self-interest and duty. At times, these economic units are creative in an always developing (or at least always changing) economy. The participating persons have responsibility) but do not always live up to it) of looking to the common good. This is necessary because Solidarists deny that one can rely upon a non-conditioned freely operating market to optimizing the social weal.[1]

Solidarism, therefore, as an economic philosophy puts the good of the human person as individual and as essentially related to others at the center of interest and concern. This includes obviously, persons' economic welfare but only as necessary means for their personal, social and moral well-being. Solidarism, far from being a top-down authoritarian uniformity, seeks to build social unity from the bottom up: among persons, within and between families, in industries, communities and in and among nations. Solidarism in essence flows from the nature of persons as not only individuals but as essentially related to and needing each other. As a social philosophy it has far reaching economic implications.

From it follows the very essential principle of economic subsidiarity, that decisions should be made by individual persons or the social group closest to the situation or problem and should advance to a higher authority only if the decision is beyond the lower's power to make. The higher authority is there to help, to subsidize, and not to replace the lower. As relating to economics, the basic right to use material goods of nature resides with every individual as a human person, as an embodied spirit, a self-knowing being who functions through material means and is totally dependent on them for surviving, communicating and acting. Fundamental, therefore, to social, and economic solidarity, is the need for society to protect the right of individuals to use and possess material goods as their own and thus to foster *Private Property as a Social Institution.*

This poses a difficulty in that goods possessed as one's own seem to suggest an individual, not a social good. Property in common (communism) would seem a more social institution. Indeed that is so in many instances and in different cultures, where monastic groups or communities of families who forego individual property ownership for the sake of sharing certain basic social or religious values. The most successful and long-lasting of such societies, however, have also been celibate and foregone family living. (This, of course, is Pesch's own experience as a lifetime member of the Society of Jesus). Nevertheless, humanity's survival as well as human experience advises that property in common must be the exception and that private property is necessarily the rule.

This seeming contradiction, that the more exclusive is more social, however, disappears and its basic solidarity becomes obvious when the possessor of property is seen as a human person. That is, every human being as an embodied spirit needs material goods for sustenance and can understand and relate to other persons and act alone or in concert with others only in physical ways and by material means. As such, therefore, natural substances are there for human living and acting. Thus their possession and use are a natural and common right for all human persons. Possessing things as private property, therefore, becomes a general need and a necessary social institution, which society must foster and protect. This in turn implies the right not only to use material goods for oneself and for one's dependents but it also requires possessing enough to anticipate one's own and one's dependents' reasonable future needs. It says further that a person can occupy whatever is not used by or of use to another or which can be obtained from another.

A person can also lay claim to the improvements made to them and to the work done to them. In this sense it is fundamental to the wage contract. Thus the right to use and to own material goods as one's own in the course of one's lifetime is a natural right and it makes for the general welfare. All in all, these uses of private property tend to strengthen social bonds and certainly can foster one's intellectual and spiritual development. *In every sense, as Pesch carefully expounds, it is a necessary social institution.*

Indeed the right to property is a social right in other respects. The right to property as the right of persons requires every person's right respecting and protecting others' rights. As such too it imposes obligations to use material goods beneficially for oneself and for others, especially one's dependents. It certainly forbids using property in ways which harm others or their property. As a temporary right it implies care to preserve it for future use, if possible, and certainly not to destroy it wantonly. Again, as a right for living in this world, it does not extend beyond the grave. Bequeathing one's property is really letting it go to another to use as he, she or they will. Finally, although the right to property is not owing to the community or state but is personal, public authorities do have the right and obligation to safeguard individuals' rights to possess and use private property. No less, they have the duty to oversee its proper distribution and use. Indeed Pesch sees an intrinsic and necessary connection between the growth of private property ownership and improving civilization. All of this, furthermore, he lays out with a clarity and simplicity which disarms dispute.

But like the good Scholastic philosopher he is, Pesch points out how other than personalist theories about private or property held in common fail to explain private property as a beneficent social institution. He gives short shrift to the various legal and contract theories of philosophers like Locke, Grotius and Pufendorf. Their theory that all lands were originally held and worked in common and later distributed by public law, simply have no evidence; and they ignore the most fundamental right of every person to the use of the earth's goods. In other words, Pesch insists against them that property rights are natural rights, not rights granted by the state of any other authority. Laws relating to or bestowing property are valid only if persons have a right from nature to possess and use material goods and thus to protect them as one's own.

Darwinistic evolutionary theories of property, especially of land, have more validity since many primitive peoples did hold and work land as a tribal good. But even so, families tended to use and keep certain goods as private. Moreover, as the rapidly developing science of paleoethnology revealed, differing primitive peoples and tribes developed different patterns in the use and possession of fields, forests, mines and fishing sites. Progressive development was a fact, although not necessarily and always upward, and differed greatly from one tribe or people to another depending on history, environment, climate and culture. In most cases communal use of land was transitional and where they continued as customary usually resulted in depleting the land, forests or wildlife.

Surprising also to many current scholars, Pesch devotes much more effort — most of a chapter — to Henry George than to Karl Marx. George had a run of celebrity with his *Progress and Poverty* and *Social Problems,* both of which also ran through several editions in German. While Pesch praises him as the "keenest and most clever of modern agrarian socialists," he is mainly interested in him because George went face-to-face with Leo XIII's *Rerum Novarum* in an open letter published nationally. Pesch's principal difficulty with George is his denial of persons' natural right to property. Perhaps influence by some of the gross injustices arising from the settlement of the West, George placed the basic natural right to ownership of land in the state. To which Pesch simply pointed out that persons were in existence and using and working the land long before states came into existence. There are other more recondite points of dispute but this right to stable ownership of property is the most fundamental right and the basis of a free-enterprise economic system which Pesch is most concerned to defend.

More contemporary to his own time, Pesch axes the Marxist principle, "To each according to need, from each according to ability," with the simple observation that needs differ from person to person and thus individual determinations are at the discretion of those in authority. Workers in their turn are not likely to perform up to their abilities if all get the same shares. There is no incentive to generate any surplus value over and beyond what has been set as personal need. Finally, since common property belongs to nobody, none have an overall care of it. The 20th Century has proven Pesch a wise prognosticator.

This social wisdom is best revealed in the final section of this book where he summarizes "The Obligations and Limits of Private Property." Here economic solidarity is represented as a balance between economic freedom and economic justice together working toward the common good. Private ownership, first of all, is a right granted to all by God as creator of the universe and upon whom all depend. But first of all this condemns a greed for property especially if causing hardships to the poor and undefended. Then as with acquiring property unjustly it should not be used wantonly and destructively but to achieve more efficient production so that all may benefit. This particularly applies to sharing one's surplus with those in need. Consequently, the state or other authority may put some restrictions on using land as well as movable property respectively as to their natures and functions. In so doing the state must safeguard civil liberty and not infringe upon the natural right to acquire, use and dispose of property. All of this suggests a more than a mere materialistic view of property, but a moral view that God instituted property for persons to achieve their full development and thus their final destiny as human persons. Above all, social order implies varying personal abilities and ambitions and thus variations in the natural right to the fruits of one's efforts. Conversely, however, need must be seen in a social sense. That is, variations in sharing property and its fruits should not be such that one or more segments of society are in dire straits while others live luxuriously.

Thus, the solidarity Pesch proposes is a balance between economic freedom and concern for the common good, which translates into a willingness to accept and to abide by reasonable restraints on economic action. It includes a willingness to hear all sides of a question and to give and take with regard to incidentals but still holding to principles. Such solidarity will vary with the type and stage of economic development. But it obviously holds to the fundamentals of a free-enterprise economy. It respects freedom to try new technologies, to generate new or change old products, to enter new markets or leave old, to improve or change productive processes, to move or to enlarge productive facilities, to hire workers or to discharge unneeded ones, to lend or to borrow from another. Conversely, free-enterprise means freedom to purchase, to seek employment, to save and to invest. All of this Pesch would accept but within a framework of conventions and laws to protect property rights especially of the more disadvantaged.

Finally, one must bear in mind that Pesch's experience of the British, German and Dutch economies and an overseas view of the U. S. economy was mainly of the late 19th and 20th Century. He had enough knowledge and experience of strikes, sweat-shops, shut-downs, monopolies, depressions and the like to come to the conclusion that "capitalistic liberalism is the enemy of the wealth of nations,"[2] Had he lived through this last, not to be regretted, Century with its wars, revolutions, purgings, depressions as well as its improvement in its ability to feed a much larger population, its technology miracles and its economic transformations through the greater part of the world, he might have written with more confidence that economic freedom with more than a modicum of social common sense offered some possibilities for a better world.

Peter L. Danner
Professor Emeritus, Economics
Marquette University

Preface

'William R. Waters, "The Influence of the Encyclicals on the Socialist Theory of Social Economy," *On the Condition of labor and the Social Question One Hundred Years Later,* ed. Thomas O. Nitsch, Joseph M. Phillips, Jr. and Edward L. Fitzsimmons (Lewiston: The Edwin Mellen Press, 1994), 484.

² p. 101

Chapter 1

WHAT IS THE MEANING OF PRIVATE PROPERTY?

Author's Introduction. If a well-established political theory appears to be indispensable for a proper decision about the problems of social life, so, no less, the position of anyone will be influenced with regard to practical problems by the approach which his way of thinking has adopted regarding the institution, private property, which has come to be so vigorously contested in our time.

Some regard private property as the source of all of our social ills, and they have set their hopes on eventually abolishing it entirely, at least so far as the means of production are concerned.

Others designate private property as an inviolable right. In the name of progress they claim unlimited liberty for the owner of property. He should be the sovereign, absolute lord over the world of material goods which he calls his own.

And there are still others who regard the institution, private property, as inseparably tied to any higher culture, and as an indispensable pillar of any well-ordered form of social life in the political order. However, they recognize limits to the acquisition and use of property; they limit the arbitrary discretion of individual property owners inasmuch as they regulate their right to use it according to the principles of justice and the common good.

The following treatment will perhaps make it easier for the reader to make a choice among these different positions.

1. By private property, we mean the right of a person over a material thing, to make use of what belongs to him in an admissible manner.[1]

The particular components of this concept call for a more detailed explanation.

a) Private property is *a right*, i.e., a moral and inviolable capacity of a person. If we say someone has the right to dispose of what he has, this means first of all that he can make use of it. But not anything which a man can do is a right. Or does the robber who has a traveler in his power therefore also have the right to seize him or his possessions? By no means; mere physical power is not yet a right. On the other hand, someone may be prevented by certain circumstances, for example physically, from working on his parcel of land, even though he undoubtedly has the right to work on it. Thus there can be a right without physical force, as there can be physical force without a right.[2] Thus, the right is essentially a moral claim, an authorization, which is based in the final analysis on the necessity of the moral order, and which adapts itself to this moral order and is conditioned by the moral law in the way it is exercised. It is for that reason and for that reason alone that the right enjoys the character of true inviolability. All other persons are bound by the moral law, obligated in conscience, not to disturb us in the exercise of our rights; and we ourselves are entitled to defend ourselves against attacks by others. The recognition by the state by its positive law of a natural right is not what first gives rise to this right and its enforceability; but it guarantees the physical enforceability of it as is appropriate to the requirements of the social order. — Now we make a distinction between personal rights[3] and material ones. The former provide to the person who has the rights a claim against other persons, according to their immediate content; and the latter afford dominion over physical things.

b) The right to property is a *material right.* — The authority which makes up its content is a power to use some thing. If someone has promised another person that he will give him a certain acre of land, then the one who was given it has a *ius ad rem,* on the basis of that promise, the rightly founded hope to get that acre. However, he has at the moment still no material right to the acre itself, but only a personal right to make a claim against the one who made the promise. It is otherwise with the property right. This provides of itself a direct *ius in re* — a right of control over a physical thing.

c) Furthermore, the right of private property is the most complete material right which a person has to a thing.[4] For according to its essential content, the property right consists in the fact that someone simply owns something as "his," and that by and of itself he may exclude everyone else from it. A natural consequence of this relationship to the thing with a person is, therefore, that the owner has the thing at his disposal as "his." [5] The guardianship which holds and administers the wealth of a ward is not ownership, because the person involved holds the wealth as someone else's. One who has the right of usufruct over a piece of land possesses the parcel and has at his disposal the productive powers of the soil. However, he does not have the acreage outright as his own, and he has control neither over the substance nor over its value. The owner, on the other hand, holds the *ius perfecte disponendi de re,* in that he enjoys the most comprehensive power to use it; also he may derive from what he owns utility and its fruits in every physically and morally possible manner, and he may alter the object as he pleases, or sell it, or use it, to the extent that he does not thereby violate higher rights and the rights of others.[6]

2. In order to make possible a right understanding of subsequent discussions, we have to present at least briefly the most important distinctions in private property.

a) we distinguish first a higher property right and a lower property right, and we do so, in fact, in a twofold sense.

God alone enjoys an original, completely independent and inalienable property right over all things. Indeed, man too has a true right to property so far as other human beings are concerned. However, in his relationship to God, that turns out to be a derivative and always a dependent right, with man himself as God's steward and administrator.[7]

Then we speak also of a direct property right and of property for use, also called a higher and a lower property right. This difference does not indicate different kinds but only different components of the property right. It is not a *divisio inter partes subiectivas,* but a *divisio inter partes integrales.* For example, the foundation, the walls, and the roof are not "kinds" of the house, but its "components." Thus, even to full ownership there belongs the *dominium directum,* as also the *dominium utile.* "Direct ownership means the right to have at one's disposal the right only of the substance of the thing, by sale, destruction, or disposal (*rei vindicatio*). Therefore we also refer to that as *dominium nudum* or *nuda proprietas,* in order to indicate its separateness from the yields from the thing. At the same time such property is not without yield and therefore meaningless, because the owner has under his control the value of the thing, and he can sell that. "Use-ownership" is the right to use the thing or to derive return from it. Thus we distinguish also the right to use (*usus,* e.g. of a house) and the enjoyment of the use, or to make use of the enjoyment (*usus fructus,* e.g. of an acre of land). The right to use implies only use, but not deriving yield from it. The right to derive return, on the other hand, entitles a person to derive yield from the property in any form so long as the substance of the thing is maintained intact.[8] Since both the user and the one who enjoys the yield must receive the substance of the thing, there can be no talk of an *usus fructus* for things which get to be used up the first time they are used (*quae primo usu consumuntur*).

b) There is a further distinction between *individual ownership* and *community ownership.*

Only a rational being, a "person" can be the subject of a right, i.e., a subject with moral competence. Now, however, we distinguish between a "physical" and "moral" person. The former is a particular, individual person, whereas the expression, "moral", "juridical", or "mystical" person signifies a group of several persons who are socially bound to one another, and which is considered a unit.

Individual property, individual private ownership, is therefore the kind which belongs to an individual person. Community property, or joint ownership, on the other hand, is the kind which belongs to a community, a society of persons, in such a way, in fact, that the community of socially connected persons ranks as the subject of the property right.

By virtue of individual ownership, all other persons are excluded from dominion over a thing, and the individual private property owner is the sole lord over the object. By community ownership, all persons who do not belong to the community are excluded from the use of the thing, but not the members of the society who together are considered a unit, and who represent the "lords" of the thing and govern its use in common.

3. The *negative* community distinguishes itself essentially from the *positive* community in social property.

If the mother places a basket of apples on the table so that the children may help themselves, it will occur to no one to regard the children as the sole legal subject with regard to those apples, or as a moral person, with the legal consequence that the little "co-owners" could now make use of the fine fruits only with "a common hand." The *communio* which exists here is, on the part of the children, solely a community or an equal simultaneous authority, i.e., each has, along with all of the others, the permission to take from the basket. On the part of the apples, there is a certain community of purpose, i.e., the mother presented the apples for "her children," without assigning specifically this apple to Peter and the other to Paul. She herself does not make the distribution, but she leaves this to the children.

The same[9] applies to the so-called negative community. In social community property, there is an actual property right involving the positive community of goods, in such a way, in fact, that the community of authorized persons is regarded as a unity, and as the subject of an actual property right, so that it also has a right over the common things only as a community. Meanwhile, negative community means solely the condition of the object's being undivided, and it negates the existence of an actual property right, whether of the community or of individual persons. What is "communal" here is solely the destiny of the thing for several or for many, and, on the other hand, the right of those several or many to take from the general supply. They are authorized to do that not by virtue of a single right of the community as such over the things in question, but each individual is entitled to do so by virtue of the personal right that he enjoys.

Thus, with Schiffini[10] we could reduce the whole meaning of the expression "negative community," to the following two points:

First, the designation means primarily that no one has as yet appropriated the good or goods in question, so that the things are for the time being more like *res nullius.*

Secondly, that anyone of the several or many persons can appropriate the goods by taking possession of them, or by virtue of another legitimate title.

Thus, the negative community consists, to state it briefly, in the capacity or the authority to acquire ownership of things which rate as *res nullius.* It is not an actual benefit, but a potential ownership, whereas the property represents actual, real ownership of goods possessed in the positive community. From this there emerges yet a very important distinction. The thing, in fact, which is subject to the positive common ownership of many can not become the property of a single individual without the consent of the others. If, on the other hand, we are talking about negatively common goods, that kind of consent is not required. —

The deeper basis of the property concept as developed briefly here will come from the discussions which are to follow. But first we will devote our attention to checking the most important opinions about the origin of private property.

¹That is "private property" in the subjective sense. In the objective sense, we understand by "property" the thing itself over which someone has command as his own in every permissible manner. — S. Schiffini S. J. defines property: "*Ius priprietatis reale perfecte disponendi de re aliqua, nisi aliunde prohibeatur.* Cf. *Disputationes philosophiae moralis* II (Augustae Taurinorum 1891), 126.

²Alois Taparelli S. J.*Versuch eines auf Erfahrung begründeten Naturrechts.* Transl. from Italian by Dr. Fridolin Schöttle and Dr. Karl Rinecker. I (Regensburg 1845), Nr. 342, p. 138.

³We may also call "personal" rights those which are associated directly with one's own person, as, for example, the right to honor and one's good name, the right to life, etc.

⁴Roman law distinguishes five kinds of material rights: *dominium, servitus, pignus, ius hereditarium, possessio iuridica.*

⁵Cf. Molina, *De iustitia et iure. Tract. 2, disp. 3, n.5.*

"*Primo quidem, quoniam recte dicimus, quia Petrus est dominus huius rei, habet facultatem perfecte de illa disponendi: e contrario vero non recte dicimus, quia habet facultatem perfecte disponendi de hac re, est dominus illius, sicut etiam non recte dicimus, quia habet facultatem videndi, est homo: ergo facultas seu ius perfecte disponendi est effectus dominii, non secus ac facultas videndi est effecus hominis.*

Secundo, quia 'esse suum', seu 'proprium' aliciuius videtur correlativum domini: dominus enim est, qui habet aliquid 'suum' simpliciter....

Tertio, potest quis conferre procuratori suo, aut amico in bonum amici ius tum ad utendum re sua omnibus modis, quibus ipse uti potest, tum etiam ad illam alienandum et consumendum, retento sibi dominio interim, dum rem non consumit vel alienat. Ergo ius ad utendum re aliqua et ad illam alienandum et consumendum, distinctum quid est a dominio, quod in eo praecise est positum, quod res sit sua simpliciter. Confirmatur, quoniam ius ad utendum re aliqua, et ius ad eam alienandum sunt iura distincta, potestque unus idem habere multa iura circa unam et eandem rem pro diversitate obiectorum ad quae sunt ea iura. Sed ratio dominii circa unam rem est unica et simplicissima. Ergo ratio iuris ad perfecte utendum et dispondendum de re aliqua diversa est a ratione dominii.

Quarto, eo ipso quod res aliqua simpliciter est alicuius, illeque proinde est dominus illius, ex natura rei habet hic plenum et integrum ius circa illam, nisi forte, res illa devincta ad eum accederet iure aliquo in re..... Sed (ut ex emphyteutico contractu est manifestum) potest is abdicare a se totum ius ea utendi, et fruendi, eamque administrandi, et conferre illud alteri, retenta proprietate, hoc est retinendo rem illam esse suam simpliciter, ut antea erat, quod iuris interpretes appellant dominium directum. Ergo dominium et iura ad utendum et disponendum de re, quae sublatis impedimentis ex natura rei dominium consequuntur, distincta inter se sunt." Cf. Schiffini, 1, c.p. 126.

[6]As a rule, the rights of property owners are divided into 3 classes:

a) *ius excludendi,* i.e., the right to prevent any one else from doing anything which would disturb the owner in his possession and use of the thing.

b) *ius utendi, fruendi,* i.e., the right to use the thing and to derive yield from it;

c) *ius disponendi* , i.e., the right to alter the thing, to sell it, etc. (the right of disposition in the narrower, iuridical sense).

Property has also been described as *ius utendi et abutendi.* If *abuti* is understood here in the sense of "misuse," the definition would involve a contradiction, since it would also involve a right to abuse. Thus, "*abuti* " means literally also, and in fact in the first instance, the same as "to use up." In this sense the property owner undoubtedly enjoys the *ius abutendi,* insofar as higher rights are not violated in the process; and only in this sense may it be understood in the definition of property. Cf. Johannes XXII, *Cap. ad Conditorem.* III. *De verbor. signific. Extravag. tit.* XIV.

[7]Cf. Victor Cathrein S. J. *Moralphilosophie:* A scientific presentation of the moral order inclusive of the legal order. Vol. 2: *Besondere Moralphilosophie.* (Freiburg 1891) p. 245. 3rd ed. 1899, p. 309.

[8]Cf. Schiffini l.c.p. 130 ff.

[9]Obviously the comparison may not be pressed; there are also differences present.

[10]*Disputationes philosophiae moralis* II, 132.

Chapter 2

HOW DID PRIVATE PROPERTY EMERGE?
LEGAL AND CONTRACT THEORIES

1. The approaches to the origin of Private property as a social institution diverge widely.

The Legal Theory

Hobbes, the teacher of King Charles II of England, established the thesis in his book, *De Cive*, that in the state of nature everything belonged to everyone. Therefore, everyone has the right to take possession of material things at will, to wrest them from others, to use them in any way he pleases. That is why the war of all against all is the most original condition of the human race. Out of fear, and in order to protect oneself in this generalized combat, people sought out others with whom they banded together for common defense. That is how the state emerged. However, it was left to political authority to establish private ownership by positive legislation and to protect what they had established.

A similar doctrine is presented by J. J. Rousseau, Bentham, Montesquieu, Jouillier and others.[1] It became the theory of the French Revolution. This is what Mirabeau said in the Constituent Assembly: "Property is acquired by the force of law; and law alone established it." Tronchet, the author of the *Code Napoléon* acknowledged the same: "Private property owes its existence and its legitimacy solely to laws." In his *Declaration of the Rights of Man*, Robespierre defined private property as "the right of every citizen to enjoy that portion of goods which the law has guaranteed to him."

Even today, this so-called legal theory, which seeks to trace the legitimacy of private ownership solely to positive state laws, is defended by many. Thus, all consistent legal positivists must adhere to it. For, if there is no law at all aside from positive state laws, then the institution of private property also cannot lay claim to any other basis.

In Germany the legal theory was and continues to be represented especially by J. H. Fichte, A. Trendelenburg, A. Wagner[2] and A. Samter.[3] —

The legal theory is untenable for the following reasons:[4]

First: its supporters proceed from the erroneous assumption that there is no such thing as a natural law. For anyone who has accepted that, nothing but positive law remains as a "legal" basis for private property. However, reliance on a merely historical, positive law does not help much, because every state law then can only claim validity for itself if there is a natural law obligation preceding positive law which requires obedience to positive laws. Without this natural law obligation to obey, positive law is *de facto* only commanded by force. But mere force will again and again be overcome "legally" by force. In principle, therefore, the proponents of the legal theory may, according to their own viewpoint, have no basis for complaint if at some point in time a socialistic majority in the country's representative body wants to do away with private property "legally," in the same way as it was introduced "legally."[5]

Second: Some supporters of the legal theory were not a little confused by the fact which they noted, that for individual persons actual property ownership was acquired solely by positive action, e.g., by heredity, contract, gifts, etc. From this they concluded wrongly that the institution, private property, also stemmed from a positive, purely historical source.

However, we could defend the most nonsensical contradictions in thousands of other situations with a similar conclusion and opinion.[6] Thus, for example, the minority status of children toward their father would be a purely positive institution. For, without that, the time when it ceases is not precisely determined, or at best at its most extreme limit. Language would be a positive institution, for without at least tacit agreement, the sound does not give expression to ideas, etc. Thus, as everyone can see, it is an affront to the laws of logic if, from the fact that we cannot arrive at any concrete structure without positive human intervention, we draw the conclusion that every institution rests solely and completely on the positive will of man. In our question here too, we must instead distinguish the abstract from the concrete, the particular from the universal, the necessary from the accidental. Therefore private property in general, as a social institution, can be viewed as something necessary; and yet at the same time its concrete structure, one or another order of property, especially the acquisition and loss of ownership of some particular thing by some particular person, may be seen as something that is accidental, variable, and the work of concrete circumstances, historical facts.

Third: it goes against reason to maintain that property was first established by a law passed by some authority.

For, "Man is older than the state, and he holds the right of providing for the life of his body prior to the formation of any State."[7] When the first people appeared on earth, and when the first families were established, the "state" was not already present in complete form. However, the individual persons and the families which actually existed before the state, and which have to be perceived logically as prior to the state,[8] already had, by the grace of God, the right to acquire property. Aside from any state provision, the necessity and the legitimacy of private ownership already emanates from the right of self-preservation, of fulfillment, and of assuring physical existence, and especially from the purposes of the family, as we will demonstrate later. No more so than the state extends to man his purpose in life, his right to life, his individual and social nature, can it be the source of those rights which are associated with and which are a *given* of that purpose of life and with that individual and social nature. —

We could perhaps say: the goods of this earth are destined for the preservation of all men. Thus, they belong to "mankind." But now the state emerges as the official representative of "mankind." Thus, it is its purpose to undertake the distribution of goods and to establish the property right.

We reply: the expression "mankind" can be understood as a collective concept or as a generic one. But is the state the official representative of the human race? Does it have the authority to provide or withhold, or to command what man is entitled to as a man to the extent that he belongs to the human race? Perish the thought, otherwise we could also be ordered legally one day to crawl on all fours. Man as man, as a member of the race, already has the right to acquire property independently, without requiring the mediation of the state to do so.

— Yet if we take the expression, "mankind" collectively, if we understand by it all men as a unit, as a single legal subject, then we would have to first prove that God turned over the world to all people together as their collective property. That would be hard to prove; however, even if we could, it would not help. For there was never one single state which embraced all of mankind. By what right therefore could the individual state represent itself as the "official representative of all of humanity," and by what right could it exclude the other states from its goods and from its territory? According to that assumption would not all of mankind as such have to undertake the distribution, so that it would be legally correct? And would not mankind, again, be entitled at any moment to abolish the ownership which the individual state brought about, to introduce a new division of the territories, etc.?

—

Fourth: finally the legal theory contradicts also the natural sense of justice. Or who would want to wait for a decree by the authorities or a law by the state to assign ownership of a statue or of a painting to the person who made that statue or that painting? Before considering any kind of positive legislation the human intellect already makes its judgment about the legitimacy of ownership, and every honorable person would judge and condemn it as a violation of justice if a positive law by the state would not recognize the wage of the worker as his private property.[9] Thus, prior to every law of a state, a sense of justice in the intellect and in conscience has already taken private property under its protection.

2. Another erroneous approach to the origin of private property is to be found in:

The Contract Theory

This was developed especially by Hugo Grotius[10] and Samuel Pufendorf.[11] According to it, private property was introduced originally by a tacit or express contract, and it has its real legal foundation in that contract.

This theory too is untenable. First, there is lacking any positive support and any historical proof for the existence of that kind of contract. —

Furthermore, such a contract would only have been actually necessary if there had been originally positive common ownership of goods as Hugo Grotius, in fact, assumed. However, history knows nothing about a positive community of goods among all of mankind all over the earth. Nor can such a positive common ownership be proven by the rational process. From the natural destiny of all temporal goods to serve the needs of "mankind," all that follows is that every person must have the right to acquire property, but not that mankind originally had an actual collective ownership on earth. —

Pufendorf, it is true, assumed only an original, *negative,* community of goods. However, since no one was accorded by nature any particular object, so, he believed, also no one may treat anything as his exclusive property without the consent or the disclaimer of all other people regarding such property. That would be correct if that original right of people to material goods were a material right. However the right which man has from nature is not a material one assigned directly by nature and acquired directly by man with regard to some particular, concrete thing, or to the sum total of all things. Instead, it appeared as simply a personal claim to appropriate from the general and negatively common treasury of goods, and to acquire what he needed for the preservation and fulfillment of his own life.

The individual thing can of its nature not serve the needs of all at the same time. Therefore the assumption makes no sense that nature gave an unconditional right to every particular thing to all people. All that is absolute is the right in general to the necessary means for self-preservation; but hypothetically there is the right to acquire specific concrete goods. That, in fact, exists — aside from cases of the most extreme need — only under the assumption that such goods have not already been legitimately acquired by someone else. Thus, also in taking possession of a good which has no owner, the consent of other people is not needed, because until the moment that it is taken possession of, no one can claim an acquired right to this particular specific good.

Finally, according to the doctrine which we are contesting here, private ownership of some particular thing could only be rightfully established on the assumption that all persons waive their claim which they have from nature to the particular individual good. Now the fulfillment of such a condition is absolutely impossible. New people are being born all of the time. But it occurs to no one to ask these for permission to go on owning also in the future whatever property they already have. We do not propose that the later generations, as their successors, are bound by the disclaimers of the earlier ones. What is involved here is not succession to an alien right, a real legal succession, but a right that is rooted in human nature, so that it is to be found wherever we find human nature, a right which is born anew with every person. If therefore the original assignment of the human race to the possession of this earth actually has the implication and the meaning that every individual person has a real legal claim to every individual thing — a legal claim which can only be lifted by a disclaimer, then the logical conclusion would be inevitable that the permanence of the original contract could be contested by the will of every newborn person. —

It would therefore be a foolish undertaking to try to provide a solid basis for the right of private property by means of the contract theory. A contract, of whose existence no one can convince himself, of which every trace is lacking, — a contract which our reason holds to be totally superfluous, a contract which, even if it had existed could be overthrown by the equal rights of the successors of the original people, — such a contract offers in fact only the flimsiest kind of basis for existing private ownership, or rather it places its legitimacy and continuance in jeopardy at every moment. The supporters of the contract theory, in fact, sensed that themselves, so that they finally presented the consensus to the primeval contract as a natural social obligation required by world order. But if world order, or better, the social order, calls for the recognition of private property, then the alleged contract is all the more proven to be superfluous and totally meaningless. [12]

[1]Cf. S. Schiffini S. J. *Disputationes philosophiae moralis* II, 148ff. 154ff.

[2]Cf.*Allgemeine oder theoretische Volkswirtschaftslehre.* Pt. I, *Grundlegung* (Leipzig and Heidelberg 1879) p. 518ff.

[3]*Das Eigenthum in seiner socialen Bedeutung* (Jena 1879) p. 309ff.

[4]Cf. Cathrein, *Moralphilosophie* II, 222ff., 3rd ed. p. 285, 287f.

[5]Adolf Wagner certainly means that a guarantee for the permanence of private ownership "lies in the moral and intellectual, and especially, in the economic education of the people, in the moral discipline and self-control of all economic classes, and in a properly organized, efficiently functioning popular representation alongside good government....Any other guarantee of all rights, therefore also of the property right, aside from moral discipline and the education of the people and the most effective possible organization of the legislative authorities, does not exist. An abuse of this authority certainly is always possible; but that does not change the establishment of property on any other basis than the legal theory." (*Grundlegung* p. 566f.). If Wagner is trying to defend the legal theory, then, in principle, he loses the right to designate the abolition of property unconditionally as an "abuse." For, if it is the state which first establishes the property right, and if this has no other legal basis than positive law, then the abolition of property contradicts neither moral discipline nor the upbringing of the people. On the contrary, the state can require the very same obedience to this new law as it did for the first law which established the property right. Also "efficiency" cannot provide any guarantee, because opinions about "efficiency" are divided and subject to change. Furthermore, "it is certainly something different whether the people can simply say to the government: you are operating inefficiently; or, you are violating my good right, you are exceeding your authority, and therefore you have no right to command obedience." Cf. Cathrein, *Moralphilosophie* II, 225 f. 3rd ed. p. 288.

[6]Taparelli, *op. cit.* I, Nr. 404.

[7]Encyclical, *Rerum Novarum* para. 6.

[8]When we propose that the individual precedes the state also "logically," all that we are saying is that one cannot conceive of the rise and the emergence of a state, without previously seeing individuals and families. — To the extent that I perceive man as intended by nature for society, the whole precedes the parts. So too the painter has in the first instance the intention of painting an entire picture. In doing this, though, the parts come first, and then the whole. No person is fully self-sufficient in himself, but he is instead dependent on society and ought to belong to it as a part of it. In that sense then, in the intention of nature society is prior to the individual person.

[9]Cf. Card. de Lugo, *De Iustitia et Iure* d. 6, *n.* 4.

[10]*De Iure Belli et Pacis* II, c.2, §2, n.5.

[11]*Ius Naturae et Gentium* 1. 4, c. 14.

[12]Cf. *Die sociale Frage beleuchtet durch die "Stimmen aus Maria-Laach,"* I, vol. 1; Theodore Meyer S. J., *Die Arbeiterfrage und die christlich-ethischen Socialprincipien* (3rd ed., Freiburg 1895) p. 101.

Chapter 3

THE ORIGIN OF PRIVATE PROPERTY ACCORDING TO THE DARWINISTIC-SOCIALISTIC THEORY OF EVOLUTION

1. We have regarded it, not without fairness, as the special accomplishment of our time that scientific investigation has paid special attention to the knowledge of the *becoming* of things. However, we need to fear that the one-sided overemphasis in this effort, which leads not infrequently to abandoning the proper knowledge of *being*, causes greater damage than the genetic understanding offers advantages. Thus, in modern philosophy we seldom devote attention any more to the search for truth, but solely, or at least mainly to the history of philosophical systems. Jurisprudence is dominated by positivism in law, and economics, in part, by a one-sided historicism. In the natural sciences, Darwinism plays its role; and scientific socialism still hopes for salvation from "evolution according to natural necessity" of the social body. Thus, it believes itself to be standing at the peak of present-day science if it progresses to the proposition that nothing is absolute and permanent, and everything is only relative and transitory. Private property in particular appears to it solely as a historical step, a "historical category" (Lassalle), a stage of development which appeared only to disappear in the course of time in the face of new structures of progressive evolution. —

It was not enough for the enthusiastic supporters of the evolutionary idea to establish the evolution of the human race on a historical basis. They went further and discovered the so-called "prehistoric" science.[1] Without reservation it is admitted that a shroud covers the history of primeval humanity, which enlightened research can from time to time ventilate, but cannot remove. But, so what? The thicker the shroud, the keener prehistoric science is, and the freer the course for the happy play of an exuberant fantasy. So let us take a walk through the beloved meadowlands of that broad field of research in the company of a representative of *extreme* evolutionism.[2] Then we may perhaps be able to congratulate the historical science for the fact that it has "since the start of the 1860's" been able to free itself from the "influence of the five Books of Moses."[3] Indeed, an entirely new and bright shining light has spread itself since that time over the origin of the family and, along with it, of private property. —

2. The cultural historical schema which, for example, Friedrich Engels establishes in the company of Lewis Morgan, lets people move through the period of savagery and then barbarism to that civilization whereby savagery and barbarism again break down into a lower, a middle, and a higher stage. Within this framework, the family, the state, and private property emerged.

In the "original forest" conditions of the lowest level of savagery, absolute promiscuity was rampant in sex life. Then there followed the family related by blood with sexual intercourse between brothers and sister, male and female cousins, but not between parents and their children. To be sure, history tells us nothing about that state of affairs; but Moran believes that he can arrive at conclusions about it from the kinship system as it is supposedly found in Hawaii and Polynesia.

In the second form of the family, sexual intercourse between brothers and sisters is excluded. It is the group marriage (Hawaiian: *Punalau* = partner), whereby the sisters in fact have men in common and the brothers have women in common., but where there is no mixing of blood between brothers and sisters. For the existence of this form of family, Morgan appeals to the organization of clans as it is found in America. The Punalua-family can supposedly even be substantiated directly in Hawaii. Engels felt that it was possible to find a throwback to the group marriage, etc. in the so-called *ius primae noctis*.

During the period of savagery where promiscuity, and families of blood relatives and groups prevailed, the right of the mother — matriarchy — applied.[4] After the mother, the descendants came next, because it was not certain who the father was. Thus, the mother stood as the head of the family, and even of the tribe, the *gens;* this was a broader circle of blood relatives of the female lineage. From those matriarchal tribes, primitive society was established. Closely tied to sexual communism was the *communism in the economic area* within the family and the tribe. The economy was a domestic one. For Engels, the communistic domestic economy and matriarchy in the house were identical.

If group marriage was the characteristic form of family during the era of savagery, so the *Syndasmische* or mating family was proper to barbarism. It already begins at the borderline between savagery and barbarism, or at the lowest level of barbarism. The man buys or steals his woman. The relationship lasts so long as it pleases the couple. A new element was introduced into the family by the mating marriage. Along with the physical mother the putative physical father now emerged, and he also rated as the owner of the tools for work, the herds, and later, the slaves. To the extent that wealth increased, the power of the father in the family grew along with his desire not to allow his own children to move into the tribe of the mother, but rather to keep their working capacity for himself; but thereby traditional heritage was changed accordingly. According to maternal right, so long as descent was calculated only in the female line, and according to the original hereditary practice of the tribe, the tribal relatives at first inherited from their deceased tribal partners. Whatever wealth there was had to stay in the tribe. The children of the deceased man, however, did not belong to his tribe, but to that of their own mother. At first they inherited along with the other blood relatives of the mother, and later perhaps in the first line from her; however they could not inherit from their father because they did not belong to his tribe, and his wealth had to stay with this. All of that is different now.

However, the overthrow of maternal right was equivalent to the *decline of the female sex in world history*. The man took over control of the household, and the woman was degraded and enslaved, the slave of his lust and a mere tool for bringing up children. The first effect of the now established sole dominion of men manifested itself in the intermediate form that was now emerging: the *patriarchal family*. What it means mainly is not so much polygamy, but rather the organization of a number of free and unfree persons into a family under the paternal authority of the head of the family. In Semitic families, being the head of the family involved polygamy; and the unfree have a wife and children, the purpose of the whole organization being the surveillance of herds on a limited area. The essential element is the cohabitation of unfree persons in the family and paternal power. The completed type of this form of family was to be found in the Roman family. At this level, the economic unit was not the individual family in the modern sense, but the domestic commune, which was comprised of several generations or individual families. The patriarchal domestic commune with common ownership of land and cultivation in common played an important transitional role among the advanced nations and some other nations of the ancient world, between the matriarchal family and the individual family which came later. It was also a transitional stage from which developed the village or march community with individual cultivation and, first periodic, and later permanent division of acreage and meadowlands.

The monogamous family finally arose from the mated family in the intermediate era between the middle and the upper stage of barbarism. Its definitive triumph is one of the hallmarks of the start of civilization. It is based on the dominion of the man with the express purpose of procreating children with uncontested paternity; and that paternity is required because those children are expected one day to move in as the heirs in the paternal estate. This differs from the mating marriage in the far greater firmness of the marriage bond which is now no longer dissolvable at the reciprocal pleasure of both parties. Now it is only the man, as a rule, who can dissolve it, and he can expel his wife. For the man the right to marital infidelity prevails, and it is exercised ever more with the increase of social development. The unfaithful wife, on the other hand, is more severely punished than ever before. Monogamy is the first form of family which was not based on natural, but on economic conditions, namely on the triumph of private property over the original common property which grew naturally. According to Engels, and also according to Fourier, monogamy and land ownership constituted the main hallmarks of civilization; and here too Engels agreed with Fourier, in that he calls it a war of the rich against the poor. —

3. If we take a closer look especially at the economic development and the emergence of private property according to the approach of Darwinistic-socialistic theory, we recognize that our primitive ancestors in the tropical and subtropical forests — the cradle of the human race — lived in trees, and fed themselves with fruits, nuts, roots; and their abundant free time was used to develop articulate sounds — language. At that time the human scarcely elevated himself above the most highly evolved animals. There was especially no trace of any productive activity. Our ancestors took from external nature around them whatever they found useful for satisfying their wants, just as the animals do so today. Eventually, then, the differentiation appeared. Man began to distinguish himself from the beast. Whereas the animal world experienced no evolution to a higher level in the way it satisfied its wants, its more fortunate brother moved more and more from being a slave of nature to being its lord.

Here we can discern several periods.

In the most ancient stages of economic development, our ancestors moved through the forests as hunters, or they sought their meager sustenance as fishermen along the coast of the seas. There was no private property aside from the goods for consumption which were supposed to satisfy the momentary wants, and also the crude tools, the ax and the spear, and then the bow and arrow. As hunting and fishing did not afford a reliable source of nourishment, what followed at this stage, not uncommonly, was cannibalism, which is still found today among the Australians and Polynesians.

Especially in the eastern continent there were to be found many animals which could be domesticated. Small wonder, therefore, if precisely there, on the grassy plains of the Euphrates and Tigris, the Oxus and Jaxartes, the Don and the Dnieper, the first pasturing took place. With the domestication of animals, however, there came also the need to seek ever new pastures, thus, the nomadic life of the pastoral people. The ownership of land and soil could not yet emerge here. Only movable things, especially the herds, were the main object of private ownership at this stage.

The living conditions of the pastoral people are, in any case, better than among the hunting and fishing people. A return to the old forest regions from the grassy river flats was therefore ruled out. However, the population increased. The free floating pasturage soon was no longer adequate for all. People moved to the North and to the West; and since the soil there no longer provided adequate food for the herds, they moved into grain culture. From the need for fodder for the cattle, there developed therefore originally the production of natural crops by human work. Since, aside from the meat of animals, there bread also appeared now, cannibalism eventually disappeared. The nomads and shepherds became settled farmers.

That was the era from which the ownership of land and the soil eventually evolved. First the whole tribe as such took possession of an area for itself. From the collective ownership of the clan, the tribe, the domestic community, however, eventually emerged the private ownership of acreage by individual families and persons.

4. If the certitude with which these so-called "solid" accomplishments of prehistoric science are presented were a proof of their reliability, then each attempt at a proof of it would be unbearable presumption. However, one who is somewhat critically disposed and accustomed to ask for the reason for and the proof of every assertion, such a person will also not be ready to strike the sail without any further ado before prehistoric science.

If we survey the history of mankind, what strikes the eye immediately, without any doubt, is the fact of a progressive development. Not every single nation rose to a higher cultural level. Some even fell back and succumbed to misery. But overall a constant progress is apparent, whose agents are now one and now another nation. Up to that point we are also in agreement with the theory of prehistoric evolution. Where we disagree is on the following points:

first: the particular point of departure which it seeks to assign to evolution;

also: the arbitrary overall generalization of their evolutionary schema. —

The theory of evolution prides itself on being free of all "metaphysical assumptions" and of having established the evolution of mankind solely on the basis of the positive and exact sciences. However, where are the *positive* reference points for that theory? Where are the documents from which the celebrated supporters of absolute evolutionism derived their information? To deliver *direct* historical proof for their assertions — that they must waive. As Friedrich Engels says:

> Of all nations in the historic era with whom we are acquainted, not a single one is still in this primitive condition. So many thousands of years as it may have lasted, yet there is little which we can prove about it from direct testimony; but to once admit the descent of people from the animal kingdom, the acceptance of this transition is unavoidable. [5]

Thus, we are dealing here only with a conclusion from a hypothesis — a hypothesis which has been abandoned today by virtually all of the most important natural science researchers! Since the supporters of prehistoric evolution for their part do not come up with any new proofs for that "assumption," and while they instead rely more and more solely on the Darwinist natural scientists, so we for our part will also waive any refutation of the hypothesis. Anyone who wants that will find it among the many anti-Darwinist natural scientists and philosophers. [6]

But let us take a closer look at the other "indirect" proofs by which prehistoric science seeks to establish its theory of evolution.

According to the extreme evolutionary hypothesis, the formation process indicated above was not accomplished everywhere to the same level of development among the different races. Some nations did not get beyond the lowest level of economic subsistence over thousands of years in their history. They remained "primitive nations." Others eventually climbed from stage to stage for a condition that was like animal want-satisfaction, until they attained that level of material production and of refined living standards which we see in present-day advanced nations. Thus, if we want to get to know the lower levels of development, we have only to compare what are in part still primitive nations of our own time, with the advanced nations. Thereby we have the so-called *comparative historical method,* which allegedly provides the proof that mankind advanced from an original animal-like condition, from savagery and barbarism, to civilization.

We will not waste our time here with how the supporters of the absolute theory of evolution, in order to come up with "primitive peoples," impute semi-animal savagery to some of the present-day inhabitants of southern Asia, East Africa, and Australia. Astute research [7] has already placed those facile assertions in the proper light. However, we would like to at least learn how the evolutionists came to the conclusion that the Australian aborigines, the Polynesians, etc. are real "primitive peoples," and that their conditions are actually the true and universal conditions of mankind. To this answer evolutionistic science will repeat anew its little speech: "Given the descent of mankind from the animal kingdom, the assumption of this transition" from the lower levels of the primitive peoples to the higher ones of the higher advanced nations is unavoidable.[8] Now that is the logic of "scientific pole-vaulter." There are no direct witnesses for an arbitrary "assumption," and the indirect proofs are based, in turn, on an "assumption," on a wholly unproven, scientifically absolutely untenable "hypothesis."

But are we not allowing too little weight for the comparative method? Did not Freeman in his book *Comparative Politics* praise the discovery of this method as such a very important one that it merits being called one of the great turning points of our century in the history of humanity? Without a doubt science, especially philology, owes to the comparative method some of the knowledge which it could not otherwise have arrived at. Thus, by comparison we were able to determine the relationship of the various national groups: As Starcke says:[9]

> The phonetic symbols which designate certain given objects,were chosen almost entirely arbitrarily, and it is therefore improbable that that at one time two different nations established the same symbol for the same object. Therefore where there is such consensus, we may conclude with virtually unchallengeable certainty that either the one nation took over the word from the other, or that it came down to both from one and the same ancestral nation. Continuing analysis can thereby establish the word origins of such an ancestral nation. By the word supply we learn, however, which images apply to the nation, i.e., we get to known its cultural condition.[10]

Very true! But that is by no means the same case as where the Darwinistic-socialistic theory of evolution seeks to acquaint us with the primitive conditions of the whole human race, especially with the origin of the family and of private property. Here we jump eagerly from the conditions of the one or the other, or even of several tribes available for research, to the primitive conditions of the human race, even though any adequate foundation for that kind of inductive conclusion is lacking, and the *differences* in the cultural development of nations and tribes is an obvious historical fact. If evolution were based on "natural necessity," even then we would have to conclude only that under the same conditions, the same phenomena would have to emerge. But who can prove to us that the one tribe in primitive times lived under the same external conditions as the other, and as the present-day so-called primitive peoples? Add to that the fact that the assumption of an evolution by "natural necessity" is refuted by thousands of facts of history, so that the impossibility of a uniform evolutionary schema is demonstrated with sun-like clarity. Even Starcke[11] admits that, inasmuch as he wants to impose the assumption "only on a highly conditioned basis," that the original conditions were about the same for all tribes of people, and that evolution went through about the same main phases. But if the similarity in the evolution and its main phases is denied, then the highly problematical character of a conclusion from the conditions of the Iroquois, etc. carried over to the primeval history of mankind becomes immediately apparent.

The fact of a progressive cultural development within mankind is uncontested; furthermore it is certain that not all nations and tribes experienced this development to the same degree and in the same manner. Some remained behind, and some lapsed again from a higher level, as this can be determined in many cases from the historically controllable facts of the history of nations. Some authors, and Starcke belongs among these, resort the cheap amusement of misinterpreting the degradation theory, which traces certain phenomena in the lives of the so-called primitive peoples to decadence, and regards the condition of savagery as corruption. The supporters of this theory by no means believe that Adam had electric lights in Paradise, or that he had a bicycle at his disposal. The one who was expelled from Paradise, like his offspring, found not completed culture at hand; but they first had to develop it, even if their intelligence already elevated them far above the animal, and in fact, provided them with the capacity for progressive cultural development. Where "animal savagery" was allegedly to be found, it would have been decadence; and until now there is no single scientific proof that the evolution of mankind took its beginnings from such "animal-like" conditions.

5. Moreover, Darwinistic-socialistic primitive history has already shared the fate of a large number of our modern theories. All too soon the sober reality followed the original enthusiasm. Today, almost all who rank as familiar with the original family, aside from Kohler, reject the Morgan-Engels theory of original promiscuity, of group marriages, etc. Thus, Westermark, Dargun, Hildebrand, Grosse, Durkheim, Cunow, and Starcke among others. Also the "maternal right" is an item that has been given up.[12] And those parts of the theory which deal with the original economy fare no better. Or where would the proof be that all our modern advanced nations were once fishermen or hunters? Where would we find the witnesses for a "hunter era," among the ancient orientals, the ancient classical peoples, the Germanic people, the Celtic people? It is precisely the most ancient historical landmarks that show us everywhere nations which live in a certain territory and carry on at least agriculture. Along with that we find among them also some work of an craft nature, and also exchange and purchase. The historical course of evolution knows nothing about a fact that for every nation and for all of humanity there necessarily had to be, or actually were, in sequence, after a "preliminary stage" of hunting and fishing, a "period" of cattle raising in nomadic life, then agriculture, and then crafts, and finally trade. On the contrary, as a rule history knows only a more or less simultaneous course of development in the overall pattern of the various productive activities throughout the economic life of a

nation. The fulfillment of the one area always led to a fulfillment in the other area with it. That certainly does not rule out the fact that nature or the location of the country can favorably dispose and incline the national endowment and history of the inhabitants of one or the other nation toward a particular kind of economic activity. However, it is precisely this peculiarity of individual nations which breaks down once again the necessity and universality of an assumed similar scheme of evolution for all nations. Furthermore, we find there, where a particular kind of economic activity moves advantageously into the foreground, also the other kinds in an appropriate manner.

> Thus, from the Phoenicians until modern England the 'trading nations' have at the same time enjoyed an outstanding position in carrying on crafts and, to the extent that the nature of the land made it possible, there was also agriculture among the other nations. The Italian 'commercial cities' were, despite a lucrative middle-man trade, also thriving craft cities, and in agriculture on their own territories, they were far ahead of the other states.[13]

Furthermore, aside from the fact that such an evolutionary schema[14] is unprovable from history, and that it directly contradicts historical testimony — a quick glimpse at the present-day, so-called "primitive people" suffices to immediately demonstrate the improbability of such an artificial progress toward higher culture, whereby each nation is supposed to have moved successively and of necessity from being a hunting and fishing nation, to being nomadic, and then an agricultural nation, etc. The present-day "primitive people" are allegedly at a stage of development which is supposed to have been the necessary transition to civilization, an ancient phase of evolution in ancient times, also for modern cultured nations. Yet, does the situation of, for example, the American Indian have something about it that confers on it the character of a phase of evolution? No; they are, as Knies rightly points out, not a "hunter nation," or better, hordes of hunters which find themselves at a rising stage of evolution. They want to be and remain hunters, and they do not want to move to a higher "preliminary stage" of modern culture." "Whereas in exceptional cases some moved out of dire necessity and force to the agriculture which they hated and even, despite instruction and example, they nevertheless waste away more and more at the 'higher level of development;' others, after the loss of their hunting reserves prefer to dream of death."[15]

It is not only historically unfounded, and intrinsically improbable, it is finally even outright physically impossible that all nations had to pass through the "preliminary" stage of hunting, fishing, and pastoral nomadic existence before they could arrive at a higher level of culture. Fishermen and hunters, as a matter of fact, can only operate in waters that are full of fish and areas rich in wildlife. For broad expanses of even the part of the earth that was then inhabited, there were in fact hunting and fishing peoples who were simply condemned to die of hunger. But where fishing provided promising yields, it is carried on now as well as then. And where hunting is remunerative, there is never a lack of nimrods. In other words: if we hope to depict the economic development of nations, we cannot abstract from the natural differences in territories where those tribes lived, whether in the gray prehistoric period, or after a migration. The economic history of nations always changes in keeping with the territorial endowment. Thus, an approach which supposes the same scheme of stages in the economic evolution of all peoples, assumes what is untrue and impossible as true and real, namely, either the universal similarity of all territorial conditions on the whole inhabited earth, or the independence of economic development of peoples from their natural, territorial endowment. Now certain nations may have passed successively through the various "stages of evolution," first as hunters and fishermen, then as pastoral nomads, then into settled agriculture, and finally as craftsmen and commercial people. Nevertheless, these are still not universally applicable or even necessary stages for the evolution for all nations, because, in fact, not all peoples could experience the same development. Just as some tribes never attained the highest, typical stages, so among others there is lacking any positive, historical reference point on the basis of which we can assert that they were once nomads, fishermen or hunters.

Along with that, the assertion will not hold up that everywhere and of necessity private ownership was absent in the original condition, and that private ownership of movable things emerged only after a time; and then, at first, there was collective ownership of land, and only at last, there developed the ownership by individual persons of land and soil. —

6. For the assumption of an original universal collective ownership of land, social democratic or Darwinistic scholars are not the only spokesmen. G. Hanssen[16] following the Dane, Olufsen, declared in favor of the assumption of an original common ownership of land and soil among the Germanic peoples. Haxthausen too shared this view after his Russian travels (1843), with regard to the Slavs. Roscher spoke of a "universal social principle," of agrarian communism as being a level of culture between nomadic existence and stable settlement with private property. Likewise, E. de Laveleye,[17] and Lewis Morgan, whose doctrines Engels and Bebel popularized, and also Voillet, Maine, Kohler, Herbert Spencer, Henry George, Hertzka, Flürscheim, and others, supported the same viewpoint.[18] According to H. Brunner[19] the "the science of comparative law presented communal land ownership

as a prehistoric institution that applied universally." However, Felix Rachfahl[20] was entirely correct in characterizing the dangers and the unreliability of such prehistoric research which "dips into the fog that covers the beginnings of human cultural life in order to make out the dull outlines in the uncertain twilight, of the most ancient institutions in the state, in law, in society, and in economic life. "It is only in most recent times that research has begun without being misled by prejudgment and unfounded generalizations, to lead toward resolving the problems of prehistoric times.

This history of mankind begins in the Orient. We have reliable reports about the most ancient conditions among the Israelites, the Egyptians, the Assyrians, and the Babylonians. There is nowhere any trace of primitive animal-origins. And there is no supporting evidence that those people first engaged in hunting, and that they then moved about as nomads, until they finally emerged as settled agricultural peoples, from where they moved on to the higher stages of culture. However, there is also no proof anywhere that there was originally and everywhere a social-collective ownership of land and the soil, or of the tools of production, from the abandonment of which private ownership first developed. On the contrary, the Bible tells of Cain having already engaged in agriculture, and also Noah. [21]

Two thousand years before Christ, Abraham purchased for a price of 400 shekels of silver from Ephron, the son of Seor, a one-acre plot as a burial place.[22] The patriarch Jacob acquired by purchase for one hundred sheep a field in the vicinity of the city of Salem, where he pitched his tent.[23] Some 500 years later this acreage was called the hereditary possession of the successors of Jacob.[24]

The Bible reports about the Egyptians, that at the time of Joseph, the Egyptians, during a time of famine, sold their private property and the soil which until then had belonged to the individuals as their free property, and which was now assigned to them by Pharaoh as their fiefs for cultivation.[25] The most important Egyptologists, like Mr. Birch, Ed. Meyer, Maspero, Lenormant, among others, also agree that about the year 3000 before Christ, private land ownership was most widespread in Egypt.

As regards the Assyrians and Babylonians, the contracts made available by George Smith, Oppert, Sayce, Peiser, and Strassmaier among others, originals of which may be found in the British Museum, in the *Cabinet des Médailles* at Paris, and in the Berlin Museum, proving that in the earliest times private property existed in both countries, to such a degree, in fact, that there is no trace, no positive support for the assumption of a still earlier collective ownership of land and soil.

Nor does the position of A. v. Haxthausen, which Emile de Laveleye shares, enjoy any historical justification and basis: that the present day Russian *Mir* is a "remnant of an ancient Slavic agrarian communism." The Russian "*Mir* " is a land-owning community. According to thorough research, especially by Joh. v. Keussler,[26] there is at present no doubt that the common ownership of the *Mir* first originated during the 17th century. The peasants who were associated with the *Mir* were serfs. They had to cultivate the land of their manor lords. Along with that, they were given in return for special services to the lord, parcels of this piece of land which were occupied by the community and were periodically distributed among the individual male members of the community for cultivation on their own account. Now when serfdom was abolished in Russia in the year 1861, this land that was until then owned collectively remained as free property. The community, however, was jointly liable to the state for it, and it had to provide all lawful public payments and services of the community members, as they had previously been jointly liable for payment to the landlords.[27] In the period prior to the 17th century, only free peasants and actual slaves where known in Russia.[28] "But the peasants, insofar as they did not live on their own parcels, emerged as tenants on the lands of the Czars, the Church, or the nobility.[29]

Older than the Russian *Mir*, — collective ownership by the community — is family ownership among the southern Slavs; in Serbia, Croatia, and Monetenegro — the common ownership of the family communes (*Sadruga*),[30] which sometimes embraced several generations. The advantages of a common administration for the first clearing projects, and greater protection against wild animals and enemies may have provided the motive for these family communes. Yet, v. Keussler indicates that the importance of the *Sadruga*, also a Slavic or at least southern Slavic national peculiarity is often exaggerated.

> This is by no means the sole kind of social living among these nations; because since ancient times we find here too individual families (*Inokoschtina*) that have been scientifically researched just a short time ago by B. Bogischitsch. Studies are lacking until now as to whether the growth of the *Inokoschtina*, this embryo of the *Sadruga*, or the permanent separation of the family, as when the son marries, etc., is or was the most common.... In any case, it is a proven fact that the individual family cannot be regarded as the exception, and that it has existed since ancient times.[31]

The Celts in Ireland lived until the 7th century A.D. in a fully communistic manner involving about 16 families in pastoral activities. But once the clans had to move on to fixed settlement, because of growing numbers of people, this occurred only in villages, but in individual farms — the so-called *Tates* — which included the barns and homes along with the lands belonging to them. Thus, individual private ownership of land and the soil arises here as soon as, and directly with, the transition from pastoral economies to settled agriculture. When along with those *Tates*, which emerged as closed individual possessions bordered by hedges or ditches, there also still existed communal land that was mostly in distant mountains and swamps.[32] Some scholars are of the opinion that among the ancient Germans too, collective ownership was for a long time the exclusive form of land occupancy. Yet, this approach also calls for a certain restriction and explanation. Actual private ownership of land will not have a chance to surface among migratory peoples, i.e., during the period of their migration. Thus, so long as the German nations had not yet acquired for themselves any secure habitation, and so long as they changed their location in rapid order, there was permanent land ownership neither of the tribe, nor of the clan members. The land remained undivided inasmuch as it was conquered by a common campaign on the part of of the whole nation so that it was to some extent the fruit of common effort, and so long as it had to be protected continuously against enemies. So according to Caesar, the Germans were still pastoral nomads. The leaders even sought at the start, in the interests of being prepared for war, to prevent with all of their might the settlement tendencies of the masses of their people. At best, as this also happens among other pastoral nomads, acres were planted here and there. Indeed, according to Caesar's report it was the princes who forced the people to take over such tasks, and also to relinquish the land if a new area was chosen for habitation.[33] However, the tribes which were growing in numbers could not have enough and assured subsistence in the long run. The move was made, driven partly by necessity, to permanent settlement; and this took place in connection with the old military organization of the tribes and their division into "hundreds."

The village constituted at first, with the emergence of settlement, the leading center of economic activity.[34] In its immediate vicinity there was the farmland, and further out were the meadowlands, which eventually faded into the great forest preserves of the village march (*Dorfmark*).[35] As regards the property situation among the German village members, the opinions of scholars are divided. Haxthausen, Roscher, and others hold for not only common ownership of land and soil during the first period of settlement, but they also argue for a *periodic redistribution* of the land. According to this approach, every father of a family is assigned an equal parcel of land for temporary possession and use. Alongside this parcel of the village march which was assigned for separate use and farming, there was the real *Allemende*,[36] not only in common ownership but even undivided for common ownership and use. It included pasture and forest, river and lake, and finally also fields lying within the divided march which were left uncultivated. At the start there was an annual change of parcels of land. Each village member thereby had a claim to sharing an equal, but not any particular acreage. He would end up with his field now here, and again somewhere else. However, the frequent changing of owners did not lend itself well to the demands of a better kind of land cultivation. Therefore, the more economic activity increases in its effectiveness, the more intense personal work moves into the foreground in planting acreage; and the more the growth of population gains in importance, the more necessary the permanent application and ownership becomes in the assignment of parcels of land. Therefore the farm became more and more an autonomous economic center within the free village community, along with the farmsteads of the rest of the march members. Work impresses the individuality of its cultivator on the acreage which is now occupied and worked permanently by the same family, and it merges ever more with his farm until the bond is recognized also at law as indissoluble. "The separate use of the land and the soil by the individual member of the march, now imprinted firmly and indissolubly, has conquered."[37] Whereas common ownership of the pasture, the forest, and the roads would continue in existence for a long time, acreage assignment became hereditary or one's own property. [38]

All of that sounds very plausible. However, the most important thing is lacking: an adequate historical basis. From the fact that perhaps one can come up with examples of a similar agrarian structure with periodic reassignments of parcels the common lands in India, China, or America, it still does not follow by any means that the same development occurred among the Germans. Even less so can we appeal to the communal structure of the Russian *Mir* as analogous. For, as indicated above, the land belonging to the *Mir* was originally a part of the property of an individual landlord, to whom the community as such was liable for all payments. Therefore it was in the interests of the community here to undertake a distribution of this land from time to time in accordance with the changing ability of the various families to perform. What is decisive, however, is the fact that the most ancient German legal sources, the so-called popular law, especially the *lex Salica,* offers no pretext for the assumption that the periodic redistribution of land constituted a separate phase in the evolution of common property into the private ownership of land between the nomadic period and settled agriculture with private ownership of the land.

> The popular laws designate the settlements as occupied by tribal colleagues, of *consanguineis, cognationibus, faramannis.* They refer to these occupants also as *commarcani* or *vicini,* and then let it be known that if the death of a member without a will occurs, his estate reverts to the community, and they accord to it the right that, without its consent, none of the members can leave his estate wholly or in part to an outsider who may wander in. The

members likewise own the common forests and pastures; and there are parcels of land where several or all of them have pieces of land. However, none of the laws mention that a piece of land that is planted by one of the individual neighbors is not his fixed and permanent possession, but must from time to time be abandoned or newly divided in a certain period. Even among the few indicated portions of the *lex Salica* 27, 15, 17, 23, and 74 *Extrav.* this approach is not possible without compulsion, and inadmissible with regard to any other treatment of land ownership and its salability.[39]

Thus, we will have to assume that the Germans, as they were arranged according to tribes in the military and were also settled according to tribes in the villages, took the land into common possession; but then they soon distributed this for the most part among families, whether by lot, or in another manner. In any case, at the time of the *Volksrecht* there was among the German tribes an undeniably clearly expressed property right of families to the farm and the land belonging to it — the so-called farmstead.[40] Along with that there was also the common ownership of the march community, the common lands of the march, where the individuals had only a right to use.[41]

7. Regarding the *communism* of the older stages of society, so much has been written in recent times. But there has also been so much fantasy about it, that it is often difficult to distinguish correctly between the truth and fiction in this area. It is all the better therefore when reputable scholars treat this subject without bias and with the requisite scientific approach. Therefore, even beyond merely wishing to complete the material which we are dealing with here, it is our intention even more so to offer a concrete example of the extent to which one can approach the theory of evolution from a scientific point of view. We do so by considering Robert Pöhlmann's *Geschichte des antiken Communismus und Socialismus*.

In the first book of his aforementioned work, Pöhlmann limits his investigation to Greece. He says:[42]

If even among the Germans, despite the priceless reports of a Caesar and a Tacitus, definite results about the main basic problems of the oldest agrarian structure, about the question of the rise and development of private ownership in land and soil cannot be derived from the sources, and if to a large extent conclusions based on the analogy of primitive social conditions must to a large extent replace strict historical proof, how much more is the most extreme caution called for where historical tradition is so much more recent and diverse.

We may risk the opinion that the Greeks at first came to their later places of settlement as nomads, and that their first conditions in the new home corresponded to the needs of a nomadic people, and that permanent settlement came only gradually. If this assumption is true, then we may also trace certain basic forms of private ownership and social order to the alleged nomadic economic system. First of all, restricted pasture lands had to be established and the herds had to be apportioned accordingly. That is because the land could only nourish a certain number of cattle, and herds that are too large cannot be reconciled with that. Also, given the closed family circles of the pastoral peoples, we must assume that the pasture reserves were divided according to families and clans in such a way that a reserve served as common property; or it did so if the pasture reserve was used alternately by different tribal groups, with the tribe as the owner of the entire tribal region. The nature of this economic system did not allow a permanent ownership by individuals of land and soil.

Already because of the unavoidable change of summer and winter, pasture which forced the community to use the various stretches of the area in a fixed order that was adapted to the time of the year, and because of the whole manner and method of cultivating the land, as it brought with it a wild field-grass culture on the whole cultivatable surface in the shift from seed and pasture, this system could not be left to the discretion of the individual economic unit and the arbitrary appropriation of private ownership. Add to that the external difficulties with which the nations at this level of culture had to contend. Against the dangers by which nature threatens what is here the most precious possession, the livestock, and where hostile forces threaten survival and freedom, the pastoral people can only assure their survival by uniting the individuals into a strictly organized community which, within the solid bond of family life and the patriarchal style of the entire pattern of existence, is generally associated with a more or less communistic economy.

Common defense, common use of summer and winter pastures, and mostly also communistic acquisition for the community, communistic leadership by the tribal leadership or the head of the clan are the characteristic features of the level of evolution which we have to consider in all probability also for the most ancient Greeks. A certain communistic organization, at least the principle of common ownership of land and the soil, would therefore have to be assumed for Greece as the starting point of its social development even if, with the inducement by which the soil and the climate inclines toward permanent cultivation, and given the difficulties which are posed for the the spatial needs of a nomadic economy by the orographic fragmentation of the land and the small expanse of its level areas, this primitive condition was overcome more quickly than would otherwise be the case. Obviously we must remain aware, for all of that, that we can be dealing here only with probabilities, and that the assumption on which the developed viewpoint rests is a more or less hypothetical one. In any case a comparison of the Greek with the other Indo-Germanic languages indicates that among the primitive expressions which indicate ownership, possession, and wealth, etc. none is found which applies to land and the soil. However, what applies to the Indo-Germanic primitive era, does not necessarily have to apply also to the Hellenic immigrants in the Balkan peninsula; and the possibility that language study to date and primitive history has assumed a far too extended duration of nomadic or semi-nomadic conditions among the various Indo-Germanic peoples, must not be rejected out of hand.[43]

Yet, Pöhlmann regards it as certain[44] that among the Greeks the transition to full settled conditions occurred in a communal manner, and that the eventual settlement of the land was not something accomplished by individuals but as communities established for all vital purposes: families and clans.

This original cooperation between tribal associations and peasant settlement communities is still clearly discernible among the largest variety of Indo-Germanic peoples; and with regard to what applies to the oldest Greek village community, Aristotle already assumed an original relationship of the members of the community inasmuch as he, among other things, rightly applied the more imaginative designation of that as *homogalaktes* (milk-cousins).[45] It is very remarkable that Aristotle also established the proposition with regard to this original identity of community and tribal colleagues that the structure of the community originally covered itself with that of the tribal community, and that the entire community organization was originally a purely patriarchal one. It is a fact that also the legal forms of the Greek state from the start identified very closely with those of the family, so that the clan association, even if it later on in the form of an artificial system of fictitious tribal relationships, asserted itself until far into Greek history as an essential factor of the political order.

Later on there was ever more penetration by the territorial principle of the organization and division of the nation based on the tribal structure. But as the tribal community in the form of the peasant settlement association was originally the main support of the economic and social organization of the people once they had settled, so the decision about the mode of settlement and the division of the land and soil also came from it.

But it is a fact that significant doubts arise immediately if we ask further how and to what degree the bond of the individuals, among these unified communities that were penetrated by the sense of the innermost vital community, came to be expressed in the order of property. Did the agricultural community hold so fast to the communal economic forms of the older economic stages, that it continued to treat the fields that were occupied as common property as such? Did it assert this cooperative common ownership not only in pasture, forest, and wasteland so that it afforded to the individual only a temporary — periodically readjusted right to use also on cultivated land, from which only gradually, with the rising demands for the intensivity of cultivation and the increasing endeavor for individual productive autonomy, separate ownership emerged? We cannot answer this question out of hand with the same assurance, as we would have to do so, according to a widely prevailing viewpoint, about the historical evolution of the economic forms. As numerous as the communistic traces may be which we have established in the agrarian laws of various nations, they are still not sufficient to justify also for times of full settlement the assertion that 'collective ownership of land and the soil can be regarded as an original phenomenon of universal applicability;'[46] or, as another supporter of the same idea expresses himself,[47] — that we must see in that a 'necessary phase of evolution for society and a kind of universal law, which operates in the movement of the forms of private ownership of land.' This 'law' can only be regarded as proven to the extent that we have in mind the first beginnings of economic development generally — without regard for the accomplished stability of habitation — or as only a part of land and the soil. We assume in that, moreover, a universal applicability also for the period of fully-settled life; and if we furthermore assume for this advanced stage the continuance of collective ownership also of plow-land, then that is certainly based on a too hasty generalization, as this easily occurs with the one-sided application of the comparative approach.

We are by no means denying the great value of the comparative method. The approach which seeks to shed light by the strictly inductive method on the unknown conditions of a nation by relying on known conditions in countries with related populations, is from the start far superior to the art of deduction from vague universal notions that is still so widespread in the science of antiquity, where a real look at things is more and more lost sight of, and also where that extreme reliance on written sources whose ultimate achievement reminds us of the proposition: *quod non est in fontibus, non est in mundo.* We also do not share completely the view that the originality of private land ownership is somehow provable among the ancient peoples, and that therefore any attempt to establish the universal economic cultural history from the secondary rise of that, is superfluous. However, if we acquaint ourselves with the variety of phenomena that are available for such an attempt — the Germanic field community, the agrarian structure of the Indian village communities, the village community of the eastern Slavs (the Russian *Mir*), the family communism of the southern Slavic domestic communities and the tribal communism of the Celtic-Irish clan structure — then we will hardly yield to the expectation that from the fullness of these unique social forms, we can come up with a similar emerging original form of private property among all Indo-Germanic people after they settled down. This varied development leads to very different assumptions for nations for which the traces of an original agricultural structure have become blurred! The comparison, on the one hand, leaves us in the dark about the form of collective use of soil these nations may have started out with, with the common ownership by the family or by the tribal association; on the other hand the possibility is by no means ruled out that here too, from the moment when the personal tribal associations became material regional communities, the individual heads of families were assigned a permanent and hereditary right of ownership to individual parcels of farmland. Insofar as what applies, for example to the Germans, where we are able to trace the process of settlement to some extent, even there we encounter agrarian collective property in the well-known passages by Caesar; but these passages deal with conditions which are still far removed from the permanent settlement of the land. A few generations later, as the nation arrived at greater permanent settlement in Tacitus' time, we run into conditions which undeniably point to the presence of definite and permanent ownership rights of individual families.[48] Whereas in Slavic village communism the share of land of all community members is time and again changed by periodic new division according to the changing number of heads, so as to maintain the principle of the equal right to economic subsistence, and whereas here the shares of the deceased members reverts accordingly to the community, while every new-born boy increases the share to the community and claims an equal portion of the existing property available, there is not to be found any trace in the Germanic field community of all of that, neither of a periodic change in the numbers and size of the plots, nor of a hereditary right of all newborn boys to the common plow-land, as this would correspond to the principle of communism alone. In other words, there is no trace here of a communism in the sense of the Slavic agrarian structure.[49]

Thus Pöhlmann asks, according to what pattern are we to envision the most ancient age of national economic development, according to the Germanic one or the Slavic one? Pöhlmann believes: according to the Germanic pattern. Yet he adds:[50]

As probable as it is that already in the most ancient German farm community, where the prerequisites were present that a certain measure of independence was accorded to the individual head member of family, even here the question remains open whether those conditions were present everywhere from the beginning. It is entirely possible that where an older population did not yet undertake the work of land cultivation, where the Greek settler encountered the unharnessed forces of a wild nature, that the instinct in the national character (for individual autonomy) was paralyzed by the common struggle against the hostile forces of wilderness, and therefore the communitarian principle could persist more so than otherwise. Here, where the strength of the individual amounted to far less, not only at the start the business of clearing and removing stumps, and of artificial drainage and irrigation, but where perhaps also sowing and harvesting were the common tasks of the farm community, the individual may well not have had any permanent land ownership aside from his dwelling. — Since we are dealing here ever more only with probabilities, and with solutions which are of relative applicability, it appears dubious from the start, when Mommsen feels he can arrive with certainty at conclusions from the mere identity of the tribal community and the village, that the Greek, like the Italian village march were operated everywhere in the most ancient times 'like a house march,' i.e., according to the system of strictest field community, whose most essential traces he assumes to be the community of ownership, common planting of the fields, and distribution among the individuals in the houses belonging to the tribe, of the yield that is harvested in common.[51] Before we can accept such a full communism in land ownership and in the yield from production, and at the same time the universality of this arrangement as a fact, altogether different reference points have to be at our command, as Mommsen himself sought to arrive at from Roman legal history, at least for the ancient Roman village community.

The solidarity of private ownership, the restriction of access by the individuals, especially to hereditary and tribal lands, as this is apparent in the older Greek law, is by no means a proof of an original agrarian communal communism, and it certainly does not lead of necessity to the common ownership by the clan. In any case, the operation of property-rights among relatives in Greek law stem from the legal conditions of the household, not from the structure of the tribal association.[52] Also, the alleged right of community members to vote, and proximity rights at sales prove, as Pöhlmann indicates, nothing about the prior existence of collective ownership in land and soil.[53] "For, if the right of the village associates provided the authority to prevent the delivery of a plot of land to a stranger that is unwelcome to them, then that would explain satisfactorily the whole character of the community association from points of view which are totally independent of agrarian law."[54]

There have also been attempts to demonstrate an original state of communism from the picture which Homer drew of the patriarchal household in the court of Priamus. The court of Priamus appeared without a doubt as a sample of the so-called domestic communities, i.e., of "associations of descendants from the same tribal father, of blood relatives of the second to the third degree who dwelled in the same courts, owned land and soil communally, and lived in common from the yield of their common work."[55] However, does this prove that the domestic community must be seen necessarily as a primitive institution? There is a twofold possibility of explaining the existence of the domestic community. It could have arisen from the fact that the original assignment of lands took place not among individuals, but to the families which were living together in domestic communities. Or else, each individual associate could have been assigned an indivisible parcel as a share of the common fields, so that with growing population eventually more families worked together on a plot, — as happened, for example in Sparta, as a result of the nonsalability and indivisibility of the *chleros.*[56]

The view which the Homeric epic affords in its entirety of the life of the nation leads Pöhlmann to the conclusion that already at the time the epic originated, the remaining personal ownership had to stem on a broad scale from the land used in common.[57] The general spread of the noble cultures dependent to a high degree on the efficiency and quality of personal work in vine and in orchard growing is a certain symptom of the ancient development of private ownership of land and the soil, without which these 'individual' cultures could not have thrived. But land cultivation too certainly, by and large, outgrew the communal field forms. The requirements of a growing population for intensity in cultivation, and on the productivity of labor were obviously too great already, and the instinct for individual gain and independent movement was too developed for — at least in the more advanced areas — a communal economic organization of agriculture to still be able to meet the needs of the time. Indeed, according to the view in the Odyssey, the division of the lands at least belongs to the first acts of human settlement, and indeed undeniably to individual ownership.[58]

Laveleye[59] appeals for a proof of a relatively long continuance of the community of fields in the Hellenic world to the communistic structure in the Liparian Island,[60] which were occupied by Hellenic emigrants from Knidos and Rhodes. However the communism of the Liparians was by no means rooted in similar conditions that existed in their original homelands. There the culture was already advanced much too far for anyone to suppose the continuance of common fields for the 6th century. Pöhlmann says,[61]

In fact, the conditions of the Liparians need not be related to those of the motherland. They are fully explained from the special situation in which the islanders found themselves. In the midst of the sea dominated by the arch-enemies of the Greeks, by the Etruscans and Phoenician Semites, in one of the most dangerous outposts of the Hellenic world, constantly threatened by catastrophes as, for example, during the Middle Ages, far-off Iceland suffered at the hands of the African pirates, the inhabitants of the Liparian islands were ever-ready for combat. Indeed, there is every indication that the Greeks, from the start, seized these islands which, as watch-towers, commanded the farthest view, with the intention of carrying on a privateering campaign against the Etruscans and the Carthaginians, which at the time was regarded as an honorable occupation, and for which the Liparians were so especially suited. But if we have here a kind of corsair fortress, then the Liparian structure stems entirely from the framework of the general national development. It emerges as a *singular phenomenon*, as, for example, that West Indian buccaneer state[62] in which too, a strict military organization on the basis of piracy was combined with communistic arrangements. [63]

Certainly it is also claimed that the state-organized citizens' meals of Sparta and Crete were a remnant of a primitive agrarian community.[64] For, how could people have consumed the fruits of the country in common if they did not originally regard the country as the common nourisher of all? Pöhlmann says,[65]

At any rate we cannot deny from the start the possibility of a strictly communal economic transitional phase of Hellenic economic development. However, mere possibilities are not the issue here. Instead, proof must be provided that the common public meals can have had no other origin, and that they could only be understood in this context. Now is the inference of roots in common fields really so conclusive?

Pöhlmann denies that completely:

> In order to understand the institutions of Sparta and Crete historically, we
> must acquaint ourselves to a much greater degree than that is usually done,
> with the living conditions and consequences of the war-like social type, as
> those were analyzed more recently by Herbert Spencer.......[66] The need to
> have at one's disposal at any moment the total strength of each individual
> leads here by intrinsic necessity to the result where the strict military order,
> the 'system of regimentation,' extends far beyond the military itself and that
> it subjects all aspects of the citizens' lives to state compulsion and to state
> supervision.....*State socialism is the natural correlative of the warrior
> society type.*[67]

From this we can explain all of those facts of Spartan-Cretan history without
having to trace them back somehow to the suppositions of an agrarian communism
in primitive times.

The form which this socialistic structuring of society took on resulted
simply from the fact that in peacetime too people maintained as much as
possible the order of the military camp. And the clearest proof of this is the
Sysstitieninstitut, the common meal for all of the citizens. The purpose of
that tradition may rightly be seen as the increase in preparedness for the
march and for combat.[68] The weapons brotherhoods which camped together
in the field and which stood together in combat continue to exist as table
companionships also in peacetime,[69] whereby the military character of the
association is held together so firmly that the *polemarcs* (*Polemarchen*) act
as supervisory officials over them, and that the comrades gather with their
weapons for common meals. In the light of these facts the derivation of
Spartan-Cretan *Sysstitien System* from political-military motives appears to
be the least forced and most natural explanation.[70] At the very least, in order
to understand that institution historically, we are by no means required to
introduce any other kind of reason for their rise, so that there is lacking any
clear reference point to an association with economic conditions. The
communal fields may also have existed at the same time as the communal
fields as the example of the Doric Liparas proves. However those need by
no means always had to operate always and everywhere in a causal
relationship with the common fields. In view of the entire position which the
common meals for citizens assume in the Doric warrior state, it is by no
means probable even for Lipara that the *Systitien* there were exclusively an
effect of the common fields. They can very well even here, as the Liparian
communal fields themselves, be regarded as the outgrowth of the
organization of the community for war. — Indeed, if the *Sysstitien* in the
form in which they are encountered by us in Lipara and Crete, as also in
Sparta, would have been a universal Doric or even ancient Hellenic
institution — as people assumed perhaps since Otfried Müller —, then we
would at any rate be justified, in fact, required to deduce at once for the
countries which found themselves in the extreme conditions of the
aforementioned communities, an explanation for a motive leading to their

rise that is of a universal nature, as the economic conditions would provide. However is there even just the shadow of a proof from that assumption?

Finally Pöhlmann also rejects the conclusion which some scholars draw from the peculiarity of the Spartan-Cretan agrarian constitution with reference to a communistic agrarian system in primitive times.[71] It is especially an unfounded, hasty assertion, in view of the factual information which we have at our command[72] at present, to assert that the Spartan priests (*Hofstellen*) turn out to be state liens[73] according to the legal provisions which apply to them. In the modern view of the Spartan kingdom as a highest regulator of economic life Pöhlmann[74] sees solely

a continuation of the ancient legend-building about the model social state, Sparta. Also that approach has in common with the ancient legend that carries over into the life of ancient Sparta the same drift which depicts an ideal state according the image derived from social theory. For, consciously or not, the Platonic state of laws came to mind here undeniably — a state which in fact rests on the principle that each of its citizens who receives a share of the soil of the fatherland, is to regard that as something belonging to the community. —

8. Let us sum up in a few propositions the results of our presentation.

First: the distinction between fishing, hunting, pastoral, agricultural, industrial and commercial nations may always be suited to give expression to the varied specific facts of economic life, and it may represent a certain pattern of stages in economic development as based on productive conditions. However, the assumption that such distinctions designate, in the sense of historical economic stages, that all nations had by necessity to pass through the same evolutionary stages, cannot be proven either from direct testimony, or by the comparative historical method, or by some kinds of rational deductions.

Secondly: the most ancient historical reports already point to fixed settlement and agriculture in nations which remained in the original home of the human race, just as they show that there was private property, not only in movable things, but also in land and the soil in the gray primitive era. Thus it is not acceptable from the historical point of view to insist that collective ownership is to be designated as a form of ownership which constituted for all nations a necessary and long-lasting transitional stage to individual property ownership.

Thirdly: as regards the tribes which left the original homeland of our race, or which in later times were forced to seek new residences by the migration of nations, the first occupation of the area for settlement may well have been by the whole tribe as such. In particular cases, common fields may have prevailed for a longer period of time after settlement, with perhaps even a periodic redistribution of the land.[75]

However, among some nomadic tribes private ownership (by individuals or families) is also in evidence immediately and directly without tribal ownership as a transitional stage, as soon as the transition from the pastoral culture moved to settled agriculture. On the other hand, however, collective ownership — where it existed — changed relatively quickly into a situation where there was private ownership, at least of the farmstead.

Fourth: wherever common ownership did indeed take on the character of a lasting arrangement (e.g., in the Indian "Land of Five Rivers" in Punjab), no higher cultural level was achieved. This fact which is not contested by the evolutionists, would seem to lead to the obvious definite conclusion that collective ownership must be regarded as a hindrance to the natural development of a higher culture. —

That brings us to the correct approach to the origin of private property.[76]

[1]Men like Lübbock, Tylor, Morgan, v. Hellwald, Lippert, etc. belong here. Cf. v. Hellwald-Bär, *Der vorgeschichtliche Mensch.* 2nd ed, Leipzig 1880. — K. v. Scherzer, *Die Anfänge menschlicher Industrie,* Berlin 1883. — N. Joly, *Der Mensch vor der Zeit der Metalle,* Leipzig 1880. — Cf. also W. Schneider, *Die Naturvölker* (Paderborn 1885) p. 413ff., where extreme evolution is refuted.

[2]It is precisely its most extreme form which allows what are generally the most peculiar flaws in evolutionistic theory come to the surface.

[3]Friedrich Engels, *Der Ursprung der Familie, des Privateigenthums und des Staates* (7th ed. Stuttgart 1898) p. xi. 1ff. 9ff.

[4]Engels (*op. cit.* p. xi f.) dates the "history of the family" to the appearance of Bachofen's *Mutterrecht,* thus from 1861: "Here the author (Bachofen) makes the following claims: 1. that people originally lived in a condition of promiscuous sexual intercourse; and he labels this with the perverted expression as *Hetaerism* ; 2. that such a situation ruled out any certain paternity, so that descent could only be calculated according to the female line — matriarchal right, and that this was the case originally among all nations of antiquity; 3. that as a result of this, a high level of respect and esteem was accorded to women as the mothers, the only parents of the younger generation who were known with certitude — which, according to Bachofen's opinion led to a total rule by women (Gynocracy); 4. that the transition to individual marriage, where the woman belonged exclusively to one man, implied a violation of an ancient religious commandment (i.e., actually a violation of the old traditional claim of all other men to the same woman), a violation that had to be atoned for, or whose tolerance had to be purchased by a temporarily limited surrender of the woman."

[5]Engels, *op. cit.* p. 2.

[6]Cf., e.g., Tilm. Pesch, *Die grossen Welträthsel* II (2nd ed., Freiburg 1892) 216ff.

[7]Cf. e.g., Peschel,*Völkerkunde* (2nd ed., Leipzig 1875) p. 137ff. — Cf. E. Baumstark, *Die Volkswirtschaft nach Menschenrassen, Volkstämmen und Völkern* (in *Hildebrands Jahrbücher* V, 81ff.). — Th. Waitz, *Anthropologie der Naturvoölker,* 6 parts. Leipzig 1859-1872.

[8]Cf., e.g., Ludwig Felix, *Entwicklungsgeschichte des Eigenthums.* Part I: *Der Einfluss der Natur auf die Entwicklung des Eignethums* (Leipzig 1883) p. 10ff. Also, Part IV, first half (1896) p. 3f.

[9]*Die Primitive Familie in ihrer Entstehung und Entwicklung* (Leipzig 1888) p. 2.

[10]As here too caution is advised, cf. e.g., Gutberlet, *Apologetik* I (2nd ed. Münster 1895), 47f.

[11]*op. cit.* p. 5.

[12]Cf. *Entwicklungsgeschichte des Eigenthums* by Ludwig Felix, Part Four, first half. *Der Einfluss von Staat und Recht auf die Entwicklung des Eigenthums* (Leipzig 1896) p. 94, where we read: "The outstanding position of Bachofen and Morgan on the basis of individualized, even if numerous phenomena, of a period of matriarchal rule, which was preceded by an period of unlimited hetaerism (Bachofen, *Das Mutterrecht* [Stuttgart 1861] p. xviii), has been abandoned by the most reputable among more recent writers; and in particular the way in which Bachofen uses mythical tales to support his view, is characterized as arising from arbitrary, unscientific, and fictional inspiration. According to Bernhöft (*Ehe und Erbrecht in der griechischen Heroenzeit, Zeitschrift f. vergl. Rechtswissenschaft* XI, 338,339) the primitive family was neither partriarchal nor matriarchal; it consisted of a man, a woman and children united in one home. Cf. Heinrich Ernst Ziegler, *Die Naturwissenschaft und die sozialdemokratische Theorie* (Stuttgart 1893) p. 43f. — Westermark, *The History of Human Marriage* (London 1891) p. 55ff. 117ff. 538. — Also R. Hildebrand (*Recht und Sitte auf den verschiedenen Kulturstufen* Jena 1896) denies that promiscuity and matriarchal right was the starting point of the development of familial law, and that we must derive the existence of matriarchal conditions from the determination of relationship to the mother among primitive nations. The studies of Cunow (*Die Verwandtschaftsorganisation der Australneger.* Stuttgart 1894), and Grosses (*Die Formen der Familie und die Formen der Wirtschaft.* Freiburg 1896) have, as Rachfahl too acknowledges (*Jahrb. f. Nationalök. u. Statist.* 3rd series, vol. XIX 1900, p. 21), made it clear that among the nations which today are at the lowest level of development, the Australian aborigines, the individual family headed by the father prevails, and that marriage is generally monogamous among them, and furthermore, the matriarchal clan, where it occurs, is not a vital community, but only a nominal one whose practical importance consists solely in that it limits the choice of mates for the members of the clan.

[13]Knies, *Die politische Oekonomie* (new ed., Brunswick, 1883) p. 366.

[14]"Whether 3, 4, 5, or more stages are assumed, and whether nations accordingly went through the stages as fishermen, hunters, farmers, industrial or commercial people, or whether their rise to higher culture occurred in another manner, really does not matter. The common fallacy of all of these demarcations consists, as Karl Knies (*op cit.* p. 364ff.) indicated, in the fact that they try to measure the actual history of nations according to one schema which abstract reason has devised. Fishing, hunting, farming etc. are types, kinds of economic activities of varying exclusiveness. But they by no means represent periods, historical stages of an actual, let alone necessary, evolution. — This objection also applies to Friedrich List who distinguished five necessary stages of evolution of human economic life in the *Nationale System der politischen Oekonomie* (Edition of L. Häusser [Stuttgart-Tübingen 1851] p. 14ff. : the savage stage, the pastoral stage, the agricultural stage, the agricultural-manufacturing stage, the agricultural-manufacturing-commercial stage.

[15]Kniess, *op. cit.* p. 364.

[16]*Ansichten über das Angrarwesen der Vorzeit.* 1835/37.

[17]*De la propriété et des ses formes primitives.* First, Paris, 1874. 4th ed., Paris 1891. German by K. Bücher under the title: *Das Ureigenthum* Leipzig 1879.

[18]Cf. Victor Cathrein, *Die sociale Frage beleuchtet durch die "Stimmen aus Maria Laach,"* Vol. I, 5: *Das Privatgrundeigenthum und seine Gegner.* Freiburg 1892, 3rd ed. 1896.

[19]*Deutsche Rechtsgeschichte* I (Leipzig 1887), 63f.

[20]*Jahrb. f. Nationalök. und Statist.* 3rd series, vol. XIX, issue 1, p. 2f. According to Rachfahl (op. cit. p. 11f.) the theory which prevails until now of the rise of land ownership suffers especially from an improper application of the comparative method: "In order to establish universally valid, so-called 'laws of evolution' or to arrive at 'an evolution according to certain laws' outcomes which are provided by the history of particular nations are too hastily applied to others. In essence there are sources of three kinds which we have at our disposal to clarify problems of prehistory: first of all, the remainders of earlier conditions and institutions which have persisted into later eras; then the literary notes from the pens of observers who belong to the nations of higher cultural levels, as these still remain among the primitive nations in the present era. Such heterogeneous source material, however, requires the most careful and painstaking treatment. By its nature, it is ambiguous, and one is especially inclined to read far too much into the sources of the first and second group, so that they may be brought into harmony by force and arbitrariness with the often only incomplete and unreliable observations based on results of ethnographic research. *It is precisely such errors which weaken the entire theory of the rise of private ownership of land in many respects.* An example is provided, for example, by the farm communities in Trier, which Hanssen wrongly proposes to be remnants of the oldest farm pattern." Those farm communities (*Gehöferschaften*) are agrarian associations with common ownership of all of the land, and they are operated on the basis of lots, with changing use of the lands. Especially along the Mosel, but also elsewhere in the south and west of Germany there were such farmstead associations. Lamprecht (Deutsches Wirtschaftsleben I, 451f.) pointed out that the associations were new land-owning structures which first arose during the later Middle Ages, and Hanssen also agreed later. (Cf. *Handw. der Staatsw.* III, 728f.) "In more recent times Meitzen came upon new sources for the history of agriculture by his study of the boundary maps, — a methodical advance of the first order. Certainly the discoverer of this genial approach often went too far, inasmuch as he felt he could read too much into them; and it was for good reason that Knapp raised objections to that when he noted: 'Let us keep the circle of sources separate! Boundary maps show precisely the situation of the acreage, but the situation of humanity stems from other documents.' (Knapp, *Siedelung und Agrarwesen nach A. Meitzen,* in: *Grundherrschaft und Rittergut* [Leipzig 1897] p. 112. Cf. G. v. Below, *Hist. Zeitschr.* LXXVIII, 471ff.) Likewise, here, where we are dealing with the solution of the problem of the beginning and the oldest history of private land ownership, we may proclaim: Let us keep the circle of sources separate! Let us avoid the unjustified and too hasty resort to the comparative method! Above all, however, we must be careful that we do not give the problem an all too universal and extended application. For, actually the general problem of the rise of land ownership breaks down into a number of individual problems, if we wish to proceed otherwise toward certain results: it is especially important that we find the right answer for each race and for each nation."

[21]*Genesis* 4:2; 9:20.

[22]*Ibid.* 23:15ff.

42   Private Property as a Social Institution

²³*Ibid.* 33: 19.
²⁴*Joshua* 24:32.
²⁵*Genesis* 47:18ff.
²⁶*Zur Geschichte und Kritik des bäuerlichen Gemeindebesitzes in Russland.* 4 vols. Riga and St. Petersburg 1876-1887. — Also Joh. v. Keussler, *Der Mir*, article in *Handwörterbuch der Staatswissenschaft.* IV (Jena 1892) 1185ff. — Also Aug. Meitzen, article: *Feldgemeinschaft* III (Jena 1892) 370ff. — A kind of common ownership which occurred in Greater Poland is no more traceable to Slavic prehistory and original collective ownership, than is the Russian *Mir*. On the contrary, the arrangement clearly stems from a later period. The land belonged to a landlord, and the commune members were his serfs. Since the community as a whole was liable to the lord for dues, it divided the land among the individual members according to the number of draft animals that they had at their disposal. Thus, it was more of a distribution of burdens than it was according to the capacity of the commune members. Furthermore it was not the collective property of the community, but the private property of the landlord which was divided up. Cf. Meitzen, op. cit. p. 372. — More recently, Simkhowitsch, *Feldgemeinschaft in Russland.* Jena 1898.
²⁷Cf. M. F. le Play, *La réforme sociale en France* III (Tours 1874) 449ff.
²⁸Meitzen, *op. cit.* p. 371.
²⁹*Ibid.* p. 370.
³⁰*Ibid.* p. 1186. — The "Sadruga" is the family cooperative which is found mostly in Serbia, with common ownership by all family members of family property.
³¹*Handwörterbuch der Staatswissenschaften op. cit.* p. 1186.
³²That kind of meadow land, occupied in common, or later the cultivated wastelands, were then divided mostly into a series of individual parcels the possession of which regularly changed, in part, each year ("*Rundalnsystem*" of "*Runrigsystem* "). Cf. Meitzen op. cit. p. 372. Maine, Gomme, and Seebohm occupied themselves in studying the *Runrigsystem*.
³³Caesar, *De Bello Gallico* IV, 1; VI, 22. "They do not engage in agriculture. Their food consists mostly of milk, cheese, and meat. None of them has a particular amount of acreage or his own land, but the chiefs and the princes always assign acreage for one year to the tribes and the clans, as much as it pleases them; and they force them to settle somewhere else the next year."
³⁴G. L. v. Maurer, *Geschichte der Dorfverfassung in Deutschland* I (Erlangen 1866) I. 40. 68. — A. Wagner, *Lehrbuch der polit. Oekonomie* I (Leipzig 1886) 13.
³⁵Karl Lamprecht, *Deutsches Wirtschaftsleben im Mittelalter* I (Leipzig 1886) 13.
³⁶*Allmende* or *Allmande*, called that because they belonged to *allen Mannen*, as the common march, and they were in common ownership.
³⁷Lamprecht *op. cit.* p. 285.
³⁸From this, its origin, what was one's own is supposed to have gotten its name, "*Allod*" (a lot or property gotten by lot).
³⁹Meitzen, *op. cit..* p. 377.

[40]Cf. Inama-Sternegg, *Deutsche Wirtschaftsgeschichte bis zum Schluss der Karolingerperiode* (Leipzig 1879) p. 92ff. 100 — Waitz, *Verfassung des deutschen Volkes* (3rd ed.) p. 124.

[41]For the assumption that among the ancient Germans common fields were very widespread, even with periodic redivisions of the acreage, one relies very much on Tacitus, *Germania* p. 26. Yet, as Meitzen (op. cit. p. 378) indicates, the few words of Tacitus offer only a guess "from a scarcely understandable rendition; and at best they offer a completely unclear meaning." Dargun (*Ursprung und Entwicklungsgeschichte des Eigenthums*, in *Zeitschrift für vergleichende Rechtswissenschaft* 1884 V, 1ff.) assumes that in the earliest stages of culture individual property ownership already existed, and that the alleged common ownership at the beginnings of evolution were more a kind of regional sovereignty. Halban-Blumenstrock too (*Entstehung des deutschen Immobiliareigenthums* vol. I: *Grundlagen* [Innsbruck 1894], p. 4 etc.) knows only soil sovereighty (*Bodenhoheit*)of the people along with individual ownership; moreover he contests the possibility of deriving a completely certain knowledge from the available sources about the character of land rights in primitive times. W. Wittich (*Die Grundherrschaft in Nordwestdeutschland* [Leipzig 1896], Appendix VI: *Ueber den Ursprung der Grossgrundherrschaft* p. 104) feels free to assume that already in primitive times there was ownership of the land in Germany. The free Germans were small landlords for whom the unfree peasants cultivated the fields. The approach of Richard Hildebrand is the same with regard to the old-Germanic estates and farm structure (*Recht und Sitte auf den verschiedenen wirtschaftlichen Kulturstufen.* Jena 1896). Hildebrand contests very generally the dominion of the communistic principle at the beginning of economic development. However, there could also be no question of the existence of private land ownership at the time, but solely of a right of the tribe members to the area, a right to occupy land and to take yield from it. We may wish to reject the explanations and positive presentations of Hildebrand in many parts, but his writing has incited new examination of the prevailing theory in favor of primitive communism. — Finally, as regards Inama-Sternegg (*Deutsche Wirtschaftsgeschichte* I, 96f.) and Fustel des Coulanges (*Hist. des institutions de l'ancienne France.*, Vol. IV, Paris 1889), they are content to deny common ownership among the Franks during the period after the invasion of Gaul. (Cf. Felix Rachfahl, *Jahrb. f. Nationalök. u. Statist.* 3rd series, vol. XIX, issue 1, p. 12ff.).

[42]*Geschichte des antiken Kommunismus und Sozialismus* I (Munich 1893) 3ff.

[43]Pöhlmann, *op. cit.* 5f.

[44]*Ibid.* p. 7f.

[45]Aristotle, *Politics* I, 2,7,1252b.

[46]Maine, *Lectures on the Early History of Institutions* p. 1.

[47]Laveleye, *De la propriété et de ses formes primitives* (1891) p. 2.

[48]Cf. *Germania* c. 20.

[49]Pöhlmann, *Ibid.* p. 9ff.

[50]*Ibid.* 13f.

[51]R. G. I, 36. 182.

[52]Pöhlmann *op. cit.* p. 15.

[53]Cf. Laveleye l.c.p.381.

[54]Pöhlmann *op. cit.* p. 16.

[55]*Ibid.* p. 18.

[56]Polybius, XII, 6. — Pöhlmann *op. cit..* p. 18.

[57]*Ibid.* p. 45f.

[58]Odyssey VI, 10. — Pöhlmann *Ibid.* 45f.

[59]L. c. p. 371ff.

[60]Diodor V, 9.

[61]*Op. cit.* p. 49.

[62]Buccaneers were the shrewd pirates in the West Indian waters (2nd half of the 17th century) who stemmed from the bull hunters of S. Domingo.

[63]Some writers (e.g. Viollet, Laveleye, 1. c. p. 372) referred to the indication in neo-Pythagorean and neo-Platonic literature that at Pythagoras' bidding 600 or 2000 persons accepted the community of goods; and they felt that they could draw from this historically very unreliable fable conclusions about traces of communism, in that they presuppose that perhaps an old misunderstood tradition about the rise of individual southern Italian communities underlies such a reference. Cf. Pöhlmann, *op. cit.* p. 53. That is in fact already more of a scientific "fabrication" of communistic traces! When Aristotle reported about Tarent, that there the rich held their goods in common with the poor, inasmuch as they permitted them to share in their enjoyment (*Politics* VII, 5,5. 1320b. [ed. Susemihl]), that cannot be regarded as the remnant of an order of common ownership of property, but only as a proof of the "effect of a highly developed social sense," which included an awareness that private ownership is not only for the interest of the individual, but that it must also serve the interests of society." (Pöhlmann, *op. cit.* p. 54ff.).

[64]Pöhlmann *op. cit.* p. 58ff.

[65]*Ibid.* p. 60.

[66]*Principien der Sociologie,* D. A. III, 669ff.

[67]Pöhlmann, *op. cit.* p. 60ff.

[68]Plutarch, *Apophthegm. Lac.* p. 226f.

[69]Cf. *Dionysius* v. Hal, II, 23.

[70]Cf. also Plato, *Leg.* I, 633, a. I, 625e, and Herodotus I, 65.

[71]Pöhlmann, *op. cit.* p. 78ff.

[72]*Ibid.* p. 65ff.

[73]*Ibid.* p. 93.

[74]*Ibid.* p. 99.

[75]Roscher (*System der Volkswirtschaft* II, 231), to be sure, holds, as we have already indicated, that the periodical redistribution of the land is a universal principle of social evolution, at a particular cultural stage between the nomadic one and the stable settlement with private property.

[76]We may legitimately pass over other theories about the emergence of private ownership, which are partly erroneous, and partly irrelevant, since we dealt with them in part in refuting the legal-, contractual-, and evolutionary theories; and to some extent these will be considered later, like Locke's labor theory, and finally, in part, some immediately show themselves as fallacious without need of refutation. Thus, for example, there was an attempt to explain private property "naturally" solely from the personality of man (Fichte, Stahl, Bluntschli). The human personality requires dominion over material goods for its economic activity. However, with this incomplete and imprecise proof, there is inadequate support for the institution, private property. — The occupation theory, which traces private ownership to the act of the will of the one who first occupies the thing, confuses the acquisition of ownership with the institution of private property. — The preferred explanation of ownership today, from the development of law and from its efficiency (historical-economic theory), also resembles partly the scientific evolutionary theory which we will deal with next; but it too must be rejected insofar as it bases itself on the scientifically untenable, positivistic point of view of historicism and utilitarianism.

Chapter 4

THE ORIGIN OF PRIVATE PROPERTY ACCORDING TO THE SCIENTIFIC THEORY OF EVOLUTION

1. When Rodbertus says about the state: "It was not creation but history which produced it,"[1] we may rightly and with the same limitation say that also about present-day private ownership.

The fact that A owns that parcel of land, while B owns this parcel as his own, and the fact that one person has at his disposal large amounts of wealth, while the other has just little, — that and similar things are without a doubt not the outcomes directly of nature; but it is traceable to positive factors.

But it is not only the association of specific individual things with particular individual persons which is the result of positive factors; — also the specific characteristic of the order of private property, the particular structure and form which the property right takes on among the various nations and in successive eras of history in legislation and in life, is the product of historical evolution. The Roman legal order of property ownership obviously has a different complexion than the German legal one; and the property order of the future will undoubtedly differ in various points from that of the present. It is in this regard that we allow for history a very important influence on the configuration of the conditions of private property.

And more still! Also property as a social institution has to a large degree become historical, even though we cannot begin to imagine a primitive situation that is completely without property. We by no means deny, especially with regard to the emergence of private ownership of land and the soil, that it did not occur everywhere with the same speed, and that it emerged instead as the fruit of a longer and more varied development. Especially wherever a really satisfactory proof for original collective ownership of the tribe, etc. is produced, we acknowledge that without reservation.

However, we contest that private ownership, like its form and configuration, so also according to its existence and its essential content, may be ascribed solely to arbitrary and purely historical causes. An arrangement which is found all over the world and among all people, and which cannot be disturbed on a permanent basis by any change in different times and viewpoints, and which strikes deeper roots everywhere that we find an improving culture, — that kind of lasting and universal institution cannot have its foundation in the arbitrary will of people or in the occasional dominant power or greed of individuals or of many; and it cannot be explained fully, solely and entirely in terms of mere historical evolution. We will rather have to look for its deepest foundation in something that is necessary under the most varied circumstances and in changing times, and which solely and exclusively has permanence and operates unchanged at all times. But that is nothing other than *rational human nature*. It is for this reason that we call the doctrine which we support: the *scientific* theory of evolution. For "science" is the certain knowledge or explanation of phenomena and things in terms of their roots. It does not operate on the basis of fantasies or arbitrary indications, but with demonstrated facts; moreover it looks for the causes and bases of actual phenomena, and it is only satisfied with the knowledge of the ultimate and highest reasons.

The needs and impulses of human, individual, and social nature, the demands and conditions of an improving cultural development, and reason which knows all of that, judges and weighs it, — those are, in the fact, the bases which can first explain how private ownership took and must take on the character of a social institution; and those are the foundations of the institution, private property, which established it as a natural law institution, i.e., one that is rooted in human reason. For all of those elements eventually hark back to the will of the One who created rational human nature, with its bodily and spiritual, individual, and social wants and inclinations, and with the craving and abilities for cultural advancement. It is the thinking intellect in us which recognizes and honors in the Creator of human nature also the highest Lawgiver of human evolution, and in it and with it, the institution of private property.[2]

To better demonstrate this moral legitimacy and necessity of private property for people and for life in human society will be our next task. If the institution of private property is, in fact, rooted ultimately in rational human nature, then it is not merely "a step in historical evolution," nor a transitional phase of evolution in the history of nations. In keeping with its essential content it will instead persist so long as there are civilized people and so long as man operates according to his rational nature as a reasonable being.

2. Leo XIII establishes in the encyclical *Rerum Novarum,* On the Condition of Labor, the proposition: *Possidere res privatim ut suas, ius est homini a natura datum* — " For every man has by nature the right to possess property as his own."[3]

We will be able to convince ourselves without any difficulty of the truth of this assertion if we keep in mind both the nature of man, as well as natural conditions — the natural purpose of life in society.[4]

The natural law basis of private property stems from:

First: the laws of human nature as they exist and existed logically and actually prior to any state or tribal community, and also before any positive common ownership. But if the justification of private property stems from the laws of human nature, then the introduction of collective social ownership on a permanent basis will appear to be contrary to nature; and it will appear so more, the less it is suited to satisfy the demands of the instincts and the craving of nature. Lorenz v. Stein made the observation with regard to the Greeks, Italians, and Germans:[5]

> In them there is a wonderful instinct whose essence it is that never and in no area of their lives was what they had sufficient. They are stern in the defense of what they own; but they strive restlessly into the unknown for more. So long as their history extends, it is as if the earth will not let them rest until they own all of it. Other nations too give evidence of great world campaigns and conquests. But they had one thing in common. It was not enough for them if the entire national group won a country. They wanted a secure share of what was gained for each individual, which would belong to him. The individual with his strength and his possessions was the goal of the whole.

The quest for individual acquisitive autonomy may be especially keen among the aforementioned nations; but overall, it has been, within proper limits, a common trait of human nature from the start; and at times more slowly, at times more quickly, it made the evolution of private ownership into a permanent arrangement of social life.

Man recognizes himself as the lord of the world with regard to the material world, by God's word, and by the qualities and powers which were bestowed on him. Everything in him and around him compels the realization of this dominion, above all:

a) the instinct and the need for self-preservation. In order to sustain his life, each person needs external goods. Now if self-preservation is a natural obligation for man, as no one can contest, the man has also a natural right to the means to preserve himself. For, that for which man has an obligation, he also has a right. The obligation and the right of self-preservation therefore includes within itself also the obligation and the right to acquire, to own, and to use the necessary means for that preservation. However, these means of preservation are in large part of such a natural composition that they can only serve one person alone and, in fact, exclusively. If provision should be made for the preservation of man in a reasonable manner, then he must also have the right to exclude others from the use of those things which of their nature can only serve one alone. However the right to exclude others from the thing, as indicated earlier, constitutes precisely the essence, the *ratio formalis,* of private property. Thus the right to acquire private property and to own it flows undeniably from the nature of man and from the nature of material things together.

But the question arises, granted also that from the obligation and the right to life, there follows a right to own those things which, because of their natural limitation, can serve only one person alone, would that right and that obligation be served adequately if the individual person could only appropriate each time as much as he needs at the moment? But where are the reasons why man accumulates supplies of goods, and constantly excludes others from them, and in fact moves to the point where he makes the land and the soil into his private property?

Leo XIII comes to grips with this objection in that he:

b) derives from providence and previous planning, as natural attributes of rational man, the necessity and legitimacy of stable private ownership, specifically in land and the soil:

> For every man has by nature the right to possess property as his own. This is one of the chief points of distinction between man and the animal creation. For the brute has no power of self-direction, but is governed by two chief instincts, which keep his powers alert, move him to use his strength, and determine him to action without the power of choice. These instincts are self-preservation and the propagation of the species. Both can attain their purpose by means of things which are close at hand; beyond their surroundings the brute creation cannot go, for they are moved to action by sensibility alone, and by the things which sense perceives. But with the man it is different indeed. He possesses, on the one hand, the full perfection of the animal nature, and therefore he enjoys, at least, as much as the rest of the animal race, the fruition of the things of the body. But animality, however perfect, is far from being the whole of humanity, and is indeed humanity's humble handmaid, made to serve and obey. It is the mind, or the reason, which is the chief thing in us who are human beings; it is this which makes a human being human, and distinguishes him essentially and completely from the brute. And on this account — viz., that man alone among animals possesses reason — it must be within his right to have things not merely for temporary and momentary use, as other living beings have them, but in stable and permanent possession; he must have not only things which perish in the using, but also those which, though used, remain for use in the future.
>
> This becomes still more clearly evident if we consider man's nature a little more deeply. For man, comprehending by the power of his reason things innumerable, and joining the future with the present — being, moreover, the master of his own acts — governs himself by the foresight of his counsel, under the eternal law and the power of God, Whose Providence governs all things. Wherefore it is in his power to exercise his

choice not only on things which regard his present welfare, but also on those which will be for his advantage in time to come. Hence man not only can possess the fruits of the earth, but also the earth itself; for of the products of the earth he can make provision for the future. Man's needs do not die out, but recur; satisfied today, they demand new supplies tomorrow. Nature therefore owes to man a storehouse that shall never fail, the daily supply of his daily wants. And this he finds only in the inexhaustible fertility of the earth.[6]

Whereas the animal must be content with the consumption of present goods, man calculates the demands and needs of the future. He knows that he can take into account future needs. Indeed, he recognizes in this capacity a great advantage of his rational nature, an expression of his human dignity. Thus, rational nature also manifests to him as a requirement of prudence that he should make use of the capacity, so that as far as he is able, he will not leave his survival to chance. Therefore the human person feels himself powerfully driven by his rational nature, to assure his future. But how could he do this better than if he has at his disposal a supply of goods from which others are excluded? And how, better than by stable ownership of land and soil? There is scarcely any need for proof that reason — prudence — must impel the person now also, in fact, to provide for the future in a deliberate manner.

Let us look now at the change of fortune which man is subject to in his weakness. Sickness, strokes of fate of any kind, can befall him, lay him low, and make very difficult, perhaps even impossible, the acquisition of the means of subsistence at the moment. What would happen to him if he could not achieve permanent ownership of things which would preserve his livelihood in time of need? What would happen to him if no one enjoyed this right, if no one could command a supply of goods from the surplus of which he could provide for his needy brethren?[7]

We may look where we wish in the world — the earth which is assigned to us as our homestead. Whether we see nature as stingy or as generous, in any case the abundance of its products vary greatly, and it is very much subject to chance occurrences. It does not provide at every time and in every place that abundance of goods which we need to preserve and fulfill our lives. The land and the soil in particular calls for the *continuing* and very *assiduous* nurturing, if it is to bring forth the necessary goods for continuous preservation, assurance, and fulfillment of life. But who would be willing to expend the efforts, and that high and yet indispensable degree of care to cultivate an acre, when he knows that it can perhaps be taken away from him in a short time? No; without stable ownership of land and the soil man will not allow himself to apply the necessary care and effort on the soil that is needed to cultivate and improve it. Without special care and effort, however, the acreage scarcely yields what is required for the present, let alone the kind of surplus over present needs which could assure against future cases of need.

The ownership of a permanent supply of goods, especially of the land and the soil, as a constant flowing source of goods is therefore fully in accordance with the *natural* and *legitimate* wishes and instincts of rational human nature; — it represents the *natural* and *best* form in which the human instinct for self-preservation and fulfillment finds its application. Now, so far as material things are concerned, since nothing stands in the way of a permanent appropriation of them, man will therefore find himself in the position of having have an undeniable, natural rightful capacity in his endeavor to assure and fulfill his temporal existence, so long as he does not violate the rights of another in the process.

As indicated, that applies also in particular with regard to land and the soil. If man has a right to harvest the fruits of the tree for himself alone, then he is no less entitled to own the tree which bears the fruit. For if the fruits are indispensable for him, the same applies no less to the tree which he must care for, trim, water, and protect against the cold and damage by wild animals, inasmuch as its products are to preserve his life in the future. But if the tree is indispensable, then likewise is the piece of land in which the tree has put down its roots, and from which it blossoms forth and yields its fruit. This land must be cultivated, freed of rocks, fertilized, if I am not to subject myself to the risk that I will lose the tree and its fruits along with it.

Thus, the quest for the assurance of his subsistence necessarily leads the person to appropriating not only the fruits of the earth, but also the land and soil itself. If someone wished to contest that right, this would be tantamount to denying the natural right of the person to provide for his preservation and for his development in a reasonable manner.

c) But if man as an individual person already has the right to acquire permanent private ownership of the fruits of the earth and of the earth itself in order to preserve and improve his life,[8] then that right emerges all the more clearly if we take into account the person in his relationship to the *family*. Let us see how Leo XIII derives a proof for private property from the *natural love of parents for their children*.

> In choosing a state of life, it is indisputable that all are at full liberty either to follow the counsel of Jesus Christ as to virginity, or to enter into the bonds of marriage. No human law can abolish the natural and primitive right of marriage, or in any way limit the chief and principal purpose of marriage, ordained by God's authority from the beginning. 'Increase and multiply.' Thus, we have the family; the 'society' of a man's own

household; a society limited indeed in numbers, but a true 'society,' and anterior to every kind of State or nation, with rights and duties of its own, totally independent of the commonwealth. That right of property, therefore, which has been proved to belong naturally to individual persons must also belong to a man in his capacity of head of a family; nay, such a person must possess this right so much the more clearly in proportion as his position multiplies his duties. For it is a most sacred law of nature that a father must provide food and all necessaries for those whom he has begotten; and similarly nature dictates that a man's children, who carry on, as it were, and continue his own personality, should be provided by him with all that is needful to enable them honorably to keep themselves from want and misery in the uncertainties of this mortal life. How in any other way can a father effect this except by the ownership of profitable property, which he can transmit to his children by inheritance? [9]

In other words: it is the strict and sacred obligation of the father to provide for the raising of his children. Moreover, he is obligated by nature to do something further for the children, inasmuch as he assures their future by leaving behind an inheritance against the varying fortunes of life. That is not to say that there is an obligation for each father to leave behind for his children an inheritance or, specifically, the ownership of certain land. In this regard, Leo XIII speaks only of the natural disposition [10] of parents, which is just as reasonable and legitimate as the desire of the individual person to acquire the greatest possible security by the stable ownership of material conditions not only for momentary preservation, but for improvement and fulfillment. If no right of another person stands in the way of the fulfillment of that parental wish, then the acquisition of private property for the children will have to be recognized as in accord with nature and with the natural competence of the parents.

d) In the assumption that man, in general, may acquire ownership of material things, the justice of private ownership finds new support in the natural right of the person to the *fruit of his labor.*

If man had no ownership right to the fruits of his work, then one could take from that against his will without being guilty of any injustice. Yet, our reason tells us clearly and precisely that such deprivation would constitute, first, violence against his person, and second, robbery of that which he rightly regards as "his." — Let us assume a person who is in the service of no one as having possession of an object without any owner, e.g., a tree in the virgin forest, who took from it wood for making an arrow for himself. Now another person comes along and takes the arrow from him. Does not everyone perceive immediately that an injustice was perpetrated thereby to the one who made the arrow? — First there was injustice in the personal violence against the natural freedom and the individual autonomous acquisition by the person. For, just as I cannot force anyone, without a legitimate claim, to expend his energies in the service of another against his will, then also the subsequent use of force which places me in the position — by the willful withdrawal of the legitimate fruit, or by negating the legitimate purpose of work that was accomplished without violating the right of anyone else — of having worked against my will for someone else or of having worked in vain, is obviously a blow against justice. Therefore it would be the theft of something which a person may legitimately regard as his own. Every person is by nature the lord of his energies and talents, i.e., he can use them as his, for himself, and to his own advantage. If he is not committed to a servile relationship by which he has obliged himself to work for someone else, then he must also rank as the natural lord over the fruits of his work.

> That which I do, is entirely in my hands; for it is a part of me, because it is my operation and the operation is a part of the cause. The operation is included in the cause, stems from it, depends on it. Thus, anyone who wishes to lay a claim to the fruits of my effort would rob me of what is mine, and he would do so without having the least right to it.[11]

Therefore, if the person has completed a processing project, or is completing work on an object to which no one can lay a higher and prior claim, justice demands that the object itself belongs to him as his property, because only in that way can he maintain the lasting possession and enjoyment of the work and the fruit of his labor.

From this original natural right of man to the products of his labor which was not performed in the service of another, Leo XIII derives a clear and convincing proof for the justice of ownership, especially of land and the soil.

We find in the encyclical *Rerum Novarum*,[12]

> Truly, that which is required for the preservation of life, and for life's well-being, is produced in great abundance from the soil, but not until man has brought it into cultivation and expended upon it his solicitude and skill. Now, when man thus turns the activity of his mind and the strength of his body toward procuring the fruits of nature, by such act he makes his own that portion of nature's field which he cultivates — that portion on which he leaves, as it were, the impress of his personality; and it cannot but be just that he should possess that portion as his very own, and have a right to hold it without any one being justified in violating that right.
>
> So strong and convincing are these arguments that it seems amazing that some would now be setting up anew certain obsolete opinions in opposition to what is here laid down. They assert that it is right for private persons to have the use of the soil and its various fruits, but that it is unjust for any one to possess outright either the land on which he has built, or the estate which he has brought under cultivation. But those who deny these rights do not perceive that they are defrauding man of what his own labor

has produced. For the soil which is tilled and cultivated with toil and skill utterly changes its condition; it was wild before, now it is fruitful; was barren, but now brings forth in abundance. That which has thus altered and improved the land becomes so truly part of itself as to be in great measure indistinguishable and inseparable from it. Is it just that the fruit of a man's own sweat and labor should be enjoyed by any one else? As effects follow their cause, so it is just and right that the results of labor should belong to those who have bestowed their labor.

This is not to say that each person possesses from nature the guarantee that he will acquire by his work, in fact, immovable property. However, if he succeeds, without violation of older or higher rights, in getting such, it would be contrary to the natural law and to some extent violence against his free personality, if one sought to take what he has rightly acquired. The Pope was trying to assert nothing else, as his words indicate clearly and precisely: "*Qua ex re rursus efficitur, privatas possessiones plane esse secundum naturam.*' "Here again, we have further proof that private ownership (according to the context: private property) is in accordance with the law of nature." [13]

And who could contest the truth of this assertion? In what other manner should the first cultivator of the soil, who put in a year of tedious work to first make the acreage capable of yielding a crop, enjoy permanently the fruits of his sweat, if there is not assured to him the exclusive, permanent, hereditary possession of the acreage; in other words, what we have always designated as private property not only according to its form, but also the according to its content? The situation of the tenant differs essentially from that of the first cultivator. The tenant pays the rental for the right to use someone else's parcel of land. But he does not enter into an arrangement of personal service to the owner. Therefore the right to the product of whatever labor he applied on the parcel of land remains with him. To him belongs the harvest; and for whatever improvements and application of value extending beyond the term of the lease, he has a legitimate claim to remuneration from the owner. It is different with the first cultivator. He occupies land that is unowned by anyone, and on which no one has yet applied labor. Therefore, he also does not have to pay land rent to anyone, just as, on the other hand, there is no one present who will repay him for his efforts and their results. It is only the ownership of the cultivated land which assures to the first cultivator permanently the fruits of all of his work, the clearing, planting, etc.

Moreover, we note here also that it is not only the harvest which constitutes the "fruit" of the work, but that instead the improvement of the soil itself, and the qualities, etc. which were added to the acreage by cultivation, all represent most directly the work of the cultivator. Taparelli said,[14]

If the person has the right to his own work, then ownership extends these rights naturally also to the land and the soil; for, the acreage requires of its nature a continuing cultivation in order to enable the human race to continue its natural replacement. Those who assert, with Mirabeau, that 'at the moment when the person has gathered the fruits, land and the soil naturally revert to common ownership,' must either presuppose that the soil that was made cultivatable, the fountains, water lines, etc. are not necessary to the human race as it propagates itself, or that they are not the works of man, or that the person can take them with him after the harvest, or that others had a right to the work of the first cultivator. The first three assumptions are refuted by the facts, and the latter by the right of natural independence, by virtue of which originally every person works only for himself. Thus, the acquisition of land is natural to man; and it stems from the necessary laws of his nature, viewed in the abstract, just as the necessity of human society also stems from them.

3. The right of a person to acquire private property, moreover, stems not only from the observance of the natural right of the person as an individual and from his closer tie to the family, but it manifests itself also clearly and irrefutably:

Secondly: as a universal social necessity.

Order, freedom, peace, material and spiritual progress quite simply constitute the natural goals and purposes of life in society. In a convincing manner St. Thomas Aquinas points out how, without the institution of private property, those social purposes cannot be fulfilled: every man is more concerned with regard to managing what belongs to him exclusively, than what is common to all or many. — Human affairs will be handled in a more orderly manner if the personal concern for one's good is left up to the individual. — Thereby a peaceful relationship among people will eventually be assured inasmuch as each person is satisfied with what is his. Conversely, we see that among those who own something in common and in an undivided manner, there are frequent quarrels.[15]

We are able to treat these reasons in a twofold aspect.

The institution of private property involves important, indeed, outright indispensable assumptions of material and spiritual progress in society.

Without private property, it would be all over with social order and peace in the state.

Let us begin therefore, by checking the necessity of private ownership for the spiritual and material culture.

a) The spiritual and moral progress of a nation are advanced by the institution, private property.

We need only refer here to the historical fact that in those nations where spiritual and moral culture flourishes, which have achieved some kind of higher level of civilization, the right of people to acquire movable and immovable property is recognized, and the acquired property is safeguarded by law. Conversely, history teaches us that the nationalities which led a nomadic life and therefore could not arrive at conditions of lasting ownership of the means of production, intellectual culture always remained at a low level.

However, it is also possible to prove directly the intrinsic connection between civilization and property ownership.

The legal possibility of acquiring property and holding what was acquired, incites people to all of those virtues without which civilization cannot survive.

By the prospect of acquiring ownership, as we have seen, the person feels himself powerfully impelled to work. However work is at the same time the means toward and the protection of moral life. It is an effective instrument toward virtue, because it is in a position to inspire self-control and self-dominance in a person. It is a firm safeguard of virtue because it removes one from the occasions which present a danger to moral life. As the idleness of acreage gives way to weeds, so it also opens the heart of the person to all kinds of vices. Therefore, not only the economic advancement, but likewise the moral progress of nations is also tied to work.

Then also, thrift, to which the ownership of property incites people because it safeguards the fruits of thrift for people, is no less an important factor for moral development. A thousand opportunities for self-dominance, and thereby for self-control disappear when the person has control over only so much as he needs at the given moment.

Property, rightly understood and used according to the intent of God, also strengthens the social bonds which tie people to one another. The rich person can and should share of his superabundance with the needy, and he can demonstrate love and awaken a sense of gratitude in the hearts of the poor. It is an alien, but nevertheless no less true, notion in our present-day socially divided world that precisely the relationship of the "employer" with the "employee" can become the source of the most intrinsic and noble behavior.[16] In a communistic society, however, a basis is lacking for any kind of friendly or even familial relationships, because the office of an overseer is never in a position to take on a paternal character. On the contrary, envy between equals operates much more dangerously and with greater bitterness. Today the worker oftentimes envies his master. But he must nevertheless recognize that the employer provides his bread, so that by his ownership he is elevated above him in his social status. If private ownership of the means of production disappears, then the material basis for any of that kind of dominance disappears. And since, as a matter of fact, domination and subordination is indispensable, then envy and jealousy will poison the hearts of men to a much greater degree and on a much wider scale, and it will stifle all nobler aspirations.

That sense of freedom, of independence, and self-esteem are by no means to be taken lightly which property ownership can confer on a person, along with right and the potential to achieve a better social status by one's own power. The ubiquitous dependence on the will of the "community" on the other hand, i.e., actually dependence on the will of the person whom the community placed above the individuals as their head — a dependence which invades even the sacred domain of the family, and which embraces the means of subsistence and the use of freedom in every regard — changes the free man into a slave or a serf.

Finally, art and science thrive only where the necessary incentive is provided from outside. If the artist has the prospect of only the same wage as the craftsman, then he will scarcely apply the great diligence to his performance as is required for really outstanding work. Actually we have to offer him more than is required for merely his sustenance; in other words we have to afford him the chance of acquiring and owning property. In addition, the great masses are unable to judge art and science properly. So one could hardly expect, in a communistic society, to provide a privileged status by majority decision for the cultivators of these higher, intellectual, cultural areas.[17] On the other hand, where private property exists, there is always likely to be among the great masses of property owners one or the other Maecenas who has an appreciation and the means to support skilled and ambitious artists by lavish donations, to motivate them to produce greater works of art, etc.

b) The social necessity of private property appears even more clearly if we take into account its relationship to material progress.[18]

Material progress depends: first on the development and fulfillment of productive work; then, on the preservation and improvement of the means of production.

— Take away private property, and both of these vital wellsprings of material advancement will soon be squelched.

a) That productive labor is indispensable for the preservation of society is contested by no one, any more than the intrinsic connection between the development of productive work and the improvement of material living conditions of people is denied by anyone. On the part of the working person, however, there are specifically two conditions on which the productivity of his work performance depends essentially. First, he must be active in an occupation where his personal talents and capacities can find their more productive application; and then, the possibility of the most productive application must actually be realized, and the existing personal ability must really be put to use.

We readily admit that, even in a social order based on private ownership, not all natural talent comes to its complete fulfillment. For there are also the extrinsic conditions in which he is born and brought up that affect the person, much like storms and frost damage many a nice blossom. But what is left over thrives and grows especially to its full fruition. Thus, not every person will be able to apply all of his natural talents fully. However, those capacities and strength which he needs for his advancement will find the most favorable conditions for their full development, especially in his surroundings, in his particular family circle, and by frequent and early and constant application, etc., if not in all cases, nevertheless with a certain regularity. So if the child has grown up, there open up for him in by far the majority of cases a wide variety of occupations, among which a free choice is possible in keeping with personal dispositions. Precisely the talents which are required for the chosen occupation have been brought to their optimal development in the present kind of system. Hence, we have the inclination to the vocation, or at least the knowledge that it is there that the capacities which are present and ready for use will find their most productive and therefore most their advantageous application.

Let us assume that social ownership had suppressed private ownership; and as a consequence, there would be no more differences in class and status; so in their social and economic relationship, all people would be equal. But are they also equal according to *nature?* Would the original natural disposition be brought to the same level by that fact? Certainly not. People will always come into this world with a wide variety of natural endowments. But if communistic society would wish to remain completely loyal to the principle that social equality is necessarily tied to economic equality, then it would have to educate and bring up all members of society in the same way. For with different training it would soon be all over with social equality.[19] What would the consequence of such equal training be? Obviously it would mean the material decline of society. For most occupations of necessity call for a very specialized, often lengthy period of training and preparation. But if communistic society, forced by necessity, sacrifices it basic principle with regard to upbringing, if it allows that at a certain age a different training takes place, despite the undeniable dangers to social equality, then new difficulties arise. Most of the communistic trainees have the necessary talents for very many kinds of employment. Now who is to decide about which of these capacities are to get special training? Since, come what may, there is no prospect anywhere of greater material advantage for the individuals, most of then undoubtedly will take to the more esteemed and easier kinds of employment. And with that, society too could not survive. It requires the continuing presence of all occupations, whereas the surplus of some occupations is tantamount to a useless and harmful waste of productive manpower. Before long, what it will come down to will be introducing compulsory occupations where it is necessary to choose one person for one occupation, and to prepare another for a different occupation. Note well: we do not have the power which hereditary status-relationships exercise over people, and with which the person is familiar from his youth, — nor the moral compulsion of one's own interests, the hope to be able to use one's capacities in some kind of occupation most successfully. No, it is a compulsion of an entirely different kind — a compulsion against which the innermost being rebels, a compulsion exercised by persons who assume the power of trying to rob the members of society of such an important and essential component of human liberty as the choice of a vocation.

If only the ideal of the most productive application of the personal capacities of all members of society could be accomplished by compulsion! Nothing less than that. Along with the freedom to choose one's occupation, the worker is robbed of the joy he takes in his work. He is a more or less demoralized human being. The millions who are burdened with the lowly mechanical processes will not rid themselves of the conviction that an injustice was done to them, and that their natural talents would have equipped them and justified their having easier and more honorable occupations.

Now add to that the fact that after abolishing private property, the most effective incentive is missing which brings the person to the point where he is active with the greatest possible application of his energies within his occupation. The instinct toward fulfillment, the quest to improve his economic condition and his social status, no longer finds satisfaction. An improvement in the condition of the individual is now only still possible on the assumption of an improvement in the overall condition of all of society. Therefore, why would he exert himself in any special manner, and why should he distinguish himself from others by energetic and steady application? In fact, as people are in their preponderant majority, nothing works more to increase exertion than self-interest, the hope to improve external material and social living conditions. Even in countries where private property is still recognized, but where its general safety at law is minimal, or where an oppressive debt or tax system robs the people of the fruits of their labor, experience shows time and again that application and pride in performance diminishes. Now take away also ownership from human society, — and the wonderful advances which human work continuously accomplishes in all branches of industrial application would come to an end; and the most productive regions would soon become wastelands.[20]

The assumption is somewhat naive that in communistic society there would be an abundant number of workers who take on themselves all of that tedium which is indispensable for the advancement of material culture. Not even more powerful impulses are sufficient by themselves among people — and most people are this way — so that without the added inducement of a lasting personal acquisitive interest to overcome the craving for leisure, they would take on the difficult, persistent tasks of peasant and industrial life. Agriculture and the workshop will only then become very attractive to a man if the exclusive ownership of the objects and the results of his work remain assured, so that the industrious plowman or shop worker can close his eyes with the conviction that the price of exertion, the fruit of his sweat will redound to the advantage of those who are called to replace his own person in society. Without this prospect, despite the truncheon of the communistic overlord, they will only do so much as is necessary in order to cover their needs of the moment. Or do we really believe that the kind of active competitive zeal which inspires the present-day employer and worker to produce ever better products by applying all of their energies, could be sustained at its full potential by the praise of the overseer, or by a good mark or the other kinds of decorations given to pupils in school? By no means! By far the majority of people will become indifferent and lazy, like the slaves of ancient times, and like people where no one has the assurance that the fruit of their labor will remain theirs.

Let us turn our attention now to the second condition of material advancement.

b) Material culture is essentially dependent on the preservation and completion of the tools of production and of labor, raw materials, tools, machines, factories, etc.

Even the richest industrialist will soon be ruined economically without the economical use of work tools. But what motivates him to carry on economically with those is, in fact, that powerful force of self-interest, the instinct of economic self-preservation, the hope for economic gain. All of these incentives disappear as soon as the work appliances are taken from the individual and transferred to society. The German proverb says: *Gesammtgut - verdammt Gut* (transl. lit. " A good that belongs to the community is a good that is damned) — That is a truth which Aristotle already recognized: *Amabile bonum, cuique autem proprium*. That which is owned in common is easily neglected, whereas people take care of what is their own. Thus, what belongs to all, in fact, thereby belongs to no one. No one has a personal, special interest in it. Therefore, even the bloodiest tyranny would not be in a position to avert a universally shoddy economy, and therefore the ruin of society.

What is more, economic progress is conditioned by an orderly progress in production, and this takes place in part by the introduction of new and more advanced productive tools. The introduction of improved tools of production, however, means first of all a not insignificant increase in work. "A nation which wants to improve and to increase its national wealth by the establishment of workshops, factories, mines, streets, canals, railroads, etc., must work hard and be willing to undergo some deprivation, just as the settler in the far West had to work hard and undergo many privations if he hoped to not only perform his ongoing tasks, but also to build a street through the forest which would connect his farm with the next settlement."[21] Now in a nation with private ownership of the means of production, the adaptation to this extra labor which is associated with the new introduction of improved means of production and transportation, will encounter little difficulty. The entrepreneur is sure of his profit if he succeeds with the help of improved tools of production in providing new consumer goods, or in presenting the old established goods more cheaply and better. The workers, on the other hand, who are required to see to their earnings will not hesitate to seize the opportunity to make good use of their working capacities. But how do things stand in the communistic society?

> In the social state where goods production overall would be in common and uniformly regulated, the annual salary of the people would obviously have to be established by and distributed among the citizens by the government. Now if the government itself were to recognize that the production of some new and more advanced tools of production are desirable, so they would increase the national allotment of pay for labor; and if the people — because they cannot immediately appreciate the advantages of the planned investments — were to view the production of them as superfluous, and avoid taking the increased work load upon themselves, then the government would have no means at all to accomplish its will, as opposed to the majority of the people; and progress would have to give way. In other words, in the social state, economic progress would always be possible only if the majority of the people were to decide in favor of it, and that, as is well known, is a long tedious route.[22]

For any person who has weighed calmly and without prejudice all of these various factors, the institution, private property, emerges definitely as an irreplaceable lever for the progress of production. The right to acquire property, the certainty that one can enjoy the fruits of his own exertion, the personal interest in the outcome of work are, in fact, the most powerful incentives giving rise to the most intensive application of individual labor ability, to a restless striving for improvements in production, to a circumspect quest for the most advantageous structure, and to a zeal for the maximum possible economic application in the technical process of production.

c) The utopian, fantasy-like character of all wholly or half communistic systems emerges even more clearly if we take into account the undeniable relationship between the social order, of peace among people, and the institution, private property.

Without the property arrangement, *a peaceful and orderly living together* among people is simply impossible in the long run.

Let us assume that private ownership is abolished. Then in its place we have communism in its various forms.[23] It is either a negative or a positive communism. "Negative," insofar as the use and administration of all goods is left to the discretion of everyone, and that there is no specific and permanent subject of property. "Positive," if there is some common being acting as the subject of ownership in all goods. *Positive* communism then divides itself, in turn, into total or half communism. The former withdraws all goods without exception from individual private ownership; and the latter withdraws only a part of it, the means of production (land the soil, tools, factories, etc.), whereas the so-called consumer goods (food, clothing) remain in private ownership.

If we ignore all varieties and peculiarities, the two types remain:

The negation of all, including social property, — which we are calling here negative communism; or,

Collective ownership in some form and to some degree — in any case, the collective ownership of the means of production.

a) In the case of *negative common ownership* the world would undoubtedly destroy itself by incessant conflict and discord. And the struggle for survival would be all the more bitter and destructive the denser the population, and the scarcer the goods which are on hand to be seized. There could be no talk of orderly production. For who in all of the world would still want to cultivate the plow-land without tools, if everyone could take over the fruits and the tools? People will fight over the goods like dogs over a bone. Brutality and physical force would prevail in the world, whereas the weak person would see himself given over to misery without rights and protection.[24]

b) Positive communism recognizes the impossibility of negative communal ownership of goods. It perceives that the very many different occupations of economic life must be arranged according to a certain order, if the needs of all people are to be provided for. But it feels that such an order can only be established in a manner where all production and the distribution of products is controlled from a central position. However, even if we may admit that in this way a certain order could be aspired to in productive activities, it nevertheless is also clear that the manner and form of this order is in sharp opposition to the legitimate demands of human nature, and that it would therefore have to lead of necessity to an insuperable wellspring of dissatisfaction and conflict. "Order" in production, in this sense, aside from the rapid decrease in productive output, where the self-interest of the individual is not directly involved, will bring with it in the shortest possible time the complete dissolution of society. That is easy to grasp. One has only to reflect on the love for personal independence so deeply rooted in human nature, and on the craving for justice.

Economic independence is an essential component of human liberty. What is it that makes the lives of the inhabitants of the English work-houses so hard? Why do many prefer to experience the bitterest want, the greatest misery rather than to go into this "well organized" work-house? It is the love of freedom, of independence, which man will not surrender unless he is subjected to continuous harsh force. That is why even the kind of socialism which requires of all of its members of society without exception that they surrender the ownership of the means of production, and with that, their economic independence, will have to resort to cruel external force in order to be able to carry out its plans and to constantly enforce them after they have been carried out. Anyone who cannot call any productive goods his own today, will, out of the need to stay alive, often find himself in a condition of bitter compulsion. However, this compulsion caused by extrinsic conditions is still a very different kind than the kind which people exercise over other people. It is more necessity than compulsion; a situation which one yields to perhaps under protest, but which leaves untouched the awareness and the sense of personal freedom. Even the poorest factory worker today feels himself to be a free man who, despite all dutiful respect, still confronts his master as a contracting party. He has at least the right and, even if to a very limited scale, the actual possibility of changing his position, his employment. The worker in the communistic state lacks all of that. He is the *slave of the community,* surrendered helplessly to the will of the majority, and thus completely dependent for his everyday livelihood on the arbitrary dominion of his immediate overlord. It is true that he has open to him recourse to the higher officials. But will he find help there or even simply credibility? And if not, will it be possible for him to appeal to the whole of society with every complaint?

No. In order to be at all bearable, collective production presupposes as essential and indispensable under all conditions the condition of peerless supervisors, who are above any kind of self-seeking, full of wisdom and moderation, free of any partisanship, and dedicated to the commonweal with a heroic sense of sacrifice — all assumptions which are scarcely to be found realized together on a lasting basis, even in wider circles. And yet, without this realization on the widest scale, communism can and must lead to arbitrary rule and bureaucratic tyranny, as history has never yet seen it, and in comparison with which the domains of the notorious oriental despots appear like an El Dorado of liberty. And if the communistic state is not to turned into an oven of constantly fermenting dissatisfaction, the comrades all together must be angels, satisfied in the spirit of obedience to the world of bureaucrats — patient and without complaint; and they must undertake all of the tasks assigned to them with a sacrificial love for the community, and likewise be willing to see patiently the fruit of their sweat, the product of their hands, the "total return from labor" disappear in the pockets of the state, of society.

Like economic independence, man also demands justice for himself. Without justice, no society can survive. However, socialism is, because of its nature, forced to slap justice in the face.

Not every system of communistic doctrine rests on the "principle" of the equality of all people. The older French socialists made an effort to establish justice in the communistic social order. The newer socialism, on the other hand, sees equality only as the "goal" of historical evolution, from which it expects everything and with which it proves everything. However all agree that the "future" communistic society has to be based on the "principle" of equality, and that without this equality it would be a non-entity. Now, however, it is simply impossible, if not physically, then morally, that in human society the burdens and benefits are equally distributed. Every attempt of that kind would have to fail in the shortest possible time, because now the natural variation in the capacities and talents of the body and of the mind runs diametrically opposed to an equal distribution of burdens. But if the burdens are not divided equally, then it is also impossible to distribute the benefits equally. Indeed, the communistic systems promise that kind of equal distribution of benefits. However, it is precisely in this way that they prove anew again their absurdity, inasmuch as they want to place a more just social order in the place of one that is based on private property, at the same time that it nevertheless slaps justice in the face in a manner that scarcely the most miserable order of property could. Even the worst wage system at least allows in some way that the more gifted and more industrious worker has the right and the possibility to earn higher remuneration based on his greater ability and work. In the consistent communistic society, on the other hand, the worker walks away from the public pay window without having his "work being given its share." He gets no more than what the officials are nice enough to provide him with, for coming to grips with his "reasonable wants." For if he got more, he would secure a surplus and keep that for himself. This would imply a restoration of private capital, and class and status differences would be reintroduced, private employment arrangements could be worked out, etc. If communism as such wants to survive, then it must of necessity rob the worker of any surplus yield or surplus value over and above what is needed to get the goods for his wants, and assign it to the community. In other words: for communism it is not at all possible for the principle of right or of justice to be controlling in the distribution of products. Nothing is decisive other than the "need" of the individual. "To each according to his needs," i.e., and above all according to the size of his stomach! Furthermore, what an abyss of disgrace and humiliation — aside from a most abhorrent violation of rights — lies in the condition alone, where strange persons, officials of the state, can allow themselves to make a judgment about what "needs" everyone has, and what can satisfy everyone![25]

Is it not truly the most complete restoration of slavery in grand style, to have to work all of one's life with inevitable necessity for a particular lord, "society," to be able to work only for this one master, and to have to work precisely according to the time and at the kind of employment which that master commands — to have to work day after day without any prospect of getting the "full product of labor," — without the prospect of a just wage corresponding to the labor input, for merely a soup ration and a free place at the general public trough![26]

Third. Support for our proof from the individual and social nature of man and, at the same time, a special proof of the necessity and the legitimacy of private property is to be found, as already indicated, in the consensus of the whole human race in recognizing the institution of private property. Certainly it is obvious that an institution which was recognized always, everywhere, in all eras, and by all nations as in accordance with nature, cannot be contrary to nature. Otherwise there would be for people no possibility at all for recognition of what is reasonably and naturally just. This universal recognition which is universal in all times and among all nations will be contested only by the most imaginative defenders of the evolutionary idea, whereas it is precisely the historical science which fully supports it.

In this regard we cannot appeal to the alleged or actual "original" collective ownership of property in individual, or even in most nations. For, first of all, what is "original" is by no means always what is "natural." It is "original" for the person to be clothed in diapers, but it is not really very "natural." "That which a being has at its first emergence, constitutes the original condition; but what happens to him by virtue of his natural and full development, constitutes the natural condition."[27] Furthermore, we cannot therefore seek to recognize the "natural" in a situation which does not yet represent the natural level of development, or which has again declined from it. Finally, even among the least developed of nations there are already enough symptoms and beginnings of property ownership. So long as they live as nomads, the individual families or individuals own at least the tents, the hunting implements, and the herds. However, after they have just barely settled down, we also very soon find the development of private ownership of land and the soil. —

In conclusion, one more quick notation. Anyone who has followed our proof carefully, will scarcely be able to avoid the conviction that the institution of private property is not only in accordance with the natural law (*secundum legem naturae*), but in a certain sense it must be designated as a *prescription* of the natural law (*de lege naturae*). [28]

All of that is not to say that *each individual* person has the obligation to acquire property, to the extent that self-preservation is not directly in question. Instead we are dealing with a generic necessity, with a necessity for people and for human society in general, just as it is also necessary for mankind to enter into marriage, even though not every individual has the obligation to choose the married state for himself.[29]

[1]*Briefe und socialpolit. Aufsätze,* published by Dr. R. Meyer II, 519.

[2]Cf. Franz Walter, *Das Eigenthum nach der Lehre des hl.Thomas von Aquin und des Socialismus. Gekrönte Preischrift* (Freiburg 1895) p. 9. "It is not the state, not the contract among people who came together from their primitive condition into a civil society, which brought about property, but the will of the highest Lawgiver." Cathrein (*Moralphilosophie* II, 223) calls the theory presented by us the economic-natural law theory. It views "private property, at least on the higher levels of civilization and within certain limits, as necessary for the requisite development both of single individuals and families, and also for the whole of society, and therefore also, assuming people as they actually are, as a necessary rational order." This theory distinguishes itself essentially from "pure economic theory," which presents private ownership not as necessary, but merely as useful and efficient, and, in fact, useful solely for the foreseeable future. A. v. Schäffle who, moreover, often changes his views can be presented as a supporter of the latter theory.

[3]Leo XIII, *Rerum Novarum* para. 6 (Doubleday ed.). — The teachings of the great theologians about the right to private property is summed up briefly by Hitze, *Kapital und Arbeit* (Paderborn 1880) p. 133ff.

[4]On property ownership and supernatural revelation, cf. Franz Walter, *Das Eigenthum* (Freiburg 1895) p. 29f.

[5]*Die drei Fragen des Grundbesitzes und seiner Zukunft* (Stuttgart 1881) p. 41.

[6]*Rerum Novarum* para. 6-7. Doubleday Edition.

[7]The objection that a supply of socially owned goods is sufficient will be dealt with expressly by refutation of social property as understood in terms of socialism and communism.

[8]Cf. *Rerum Novarum*: the expressions "*conservanda*" and "*perficienda vita.*"

[9]*Ibid.* para. 12-13.

[10]*Ibid.* para. 13. "*Sanctissima naturae lex est, ut victu omnique cultu paterfamilias tueatur, quos ipse procreavit: idemque illuc a natura deducitur, ut velit liberis suis, quippe qui paternam referunt et quodam modo producunt personam, acquirere et parare, unde se honeste possint in ancipiti vitae cursu a misera fortuna defendere. Id vero efficere non alia ratione potest, nisi fructuosarum possessione rerum, quas ad liberos hereditate transmittat.*"

[11]Taparelli, *op. cit.* I, 167.

[12]*Rerum Novarum* para. 9-10.

[13]*Ibid.* para. 9.

[14]Taparelli, *op. cit.* I, No. 407.

[15]S. Thomas, 2,2, q.66, a.2. (*corpus artic.*) "*Respondeo dicendum, quod circa rem exteriorem duo competunt homini, quorum unum est potestas procurandi et dispensandi, et quantum ad hoc licitum est, quod homo propria possideat. Et est etiam necessarium ad humanam vitam propter tria: Primo quidem, quia magis sollicitus est unusquisque ad procurandum aliquid quod sibi soli competit, quam id, quod est commune omnium vel multorum: quia unusquisque laborem fugiens, relinquit alteri id, quod pertinet ad commune, sicut accidit in multitudine ministrorum. Alio modo quia ordinatius res humanae tractantur, si singulis immineat propria cura alicuius rei procurandae: esset autem confusio, si quilibet indisincte quaelibet procuraret. Tertio, quia per hoc magis pacificus status hominum conservatur, dum unusquisque re sua contentus est. Unde videmus quod inter eos, qui communiter et ex indiviso aliquid possident, frequentius iurgia oriuntur.*" St. Thomas brought up the question of property ownership "only very incidentally where the question of theft and robbery comes up in the system of special morality. Two things are missing here, first of all the very important distinction between the objects of direct consumption, and the means for economic production; then also the historical rendition of the very abstract manner of observation. The latter shows that the concept of property developed very differently with regard to the two different groups of goods." (v. Hertling, *Zur Beantwortung der Göttinger Jubiläumsrede* [Münster and Paderborn 1887] p. 16).

Also lacking in Thomas is a definition of the right of private ownership. Cf. Franz Walter, *Das Eigenthum* (Freiburg 1895) p. 6, with footnotes.

[16]Cf. *Arbeiterwohl* 1st yr. vol. I (3rd ed. Cologne 1881) p. 41ff.

[17]In fact, present-day socialism knows no scholars and artists by profession in its picture of the future. All, without exception, should devote themselves to the production of material goods. Afterwards they can compose and make music, just as even now a person can be a shoemaker all day long and then turn up for the dance after hours. Many may doubt whether this kind of system could produce a Dante or a Beethoven.

[18]Cf. Franz Schaub, *Die Eigenthumslehre nach Thomas von Aquin und dem modernen Socialismus* (Freiburg 1898) p. 269ff. 283ff. 286ff. 298ff.

[19]Present-day socialism promises seriously that in the communistic social order education and technical training will prepare everyone to work at all functions and industries. Thus, no teacher will be able to say to the mother, your son truly has a good heart, but he has little grasp. The youth of the future will know only universal genius. The principle of education: *non multa, sed multum* no longer have any application. Everyone will learn everything, and everyone will be able to do everything. That is what social equality calls for. Thus, work will naturally be equated with being able. Everyone will be employed at the greatest variety of branches. In the morning he will clean latrines, and in the afternoon he will teach about the materialistic world-view, both, naturally, with excellence. Cf. Cathrein, *Socialismus* (6th ed., Freiburg 1892) p. 160ff. (7th ed. 1898) p. 205ff.

[20]About the much praised Russian "*Mir*," those who know something about it give it mixed reviews: "The Russian commune with its common ownership is an institution which not only does not allow any wealth to emerge, but which, with the growth of population, must of necessity lead to the ruin of the farmers and the community; and indeed, conditions would also not be more favorable if the population had not moved from serfdom into the realm of unlimited freedom, so that it was left to run wild. In other countries, if an economic crisis occurs, at least a part of the peasant population could put up some resistance, while the ownership of the other portion, even if at reduced prices resulting from the depreciation of land and the soil, could find new owners, where the formerly independent peasant could earn his livelihood as a tenant or as a farm worker. In Russia the entire peasant population must eventually be reduced to a proletariat, even while we know that according to the view of those who support the commune count on it to prevent the rise of any proletariat." (A. Westländer, *Russland vor einem Regime-Wechsel* [Stuttgart 1894] p. 28f.)

[21]Schönberg, *Handbuch der polit. Oekonomie* I (2nd ed. Tübingen 1885) 259. (Essay by Kleinwächter on economic production in general).

[22]Kleinwächter *op. cit.* p. 260.

[23]Cf. Cathrein, *Socialismus* p.1ff.

[24]Lessius, *de iustitia et iure, lib.* II, c. 5. dub. 2. "*Si manissent (res) communes, mundus arderet perpetuis contentionibus et bellis; quia plerumque plures concurrerent ad eandem rem occupandam, qui se mutuo conarentur impedire: et potentiores plerumque omnia raperent. Nec meum et tuum (quae dicuntur esse potissima causa dissensionum) tunc minus fuissent, quam modo: quisque enim conatus fuisset rem communem, dum ea utendum esset, facere suam; sicque assiduo rixae et pugnae inter homines existissent.*"

[25]A level of want satisfaction "as one pleases" is out of the question in any case, or else everyone would obviously take as much for himself as he could.

[26]Schiffini I, c. p. 141ff.

[27]Taparelli, *op. cit.* I 408.

[28]A. Castelein, S. J. (*Le Socialisme et le Droit de Propriété* [Brussels, 1896] p. 511ff.) incorporates the natural law basis of the institution of private property under the threefold point of view: man is a *personal, social* being *capable of perfection.*

[29]Schiffini, 1. c. p. 146. "*Hoc porro accipi debet consimili plane ratione ac asseruimus agentes de naturali hominis sociabilitate. Quemadmodum enim lex naturae, etsi non praecipit singulis hominibus, ut sint membra societatis perfectae sive civitatis, praecipit tamen universe et in tenere, ut diversae familiae sufficienter multiplicatae in unam vel plures societates civiles congregentur: sic etiam non exigit quidem, ut singuli homines vero aliquo dominio proprietatis actu fruantur individuali aut collectivo, exigit tamen, ut in praesenti statu humani generis, et in tanta hominum multitudine, prout nunc existunt, non sit illa bonorum communitas, quam communistae et socialistae proponunt, sed dominia reum uno vel altero modo sint divisa in proprietates diversas, easque etiam privatas et individuales.*"

Chapter 5

GENERAL OBJECTIONS TO PRIVATE PROPERTY

1. The legitimacy of private property has been contested most vigorously time and again. There have even been appeals to theology and to the Fathers of the Church to show that the institution of private property is an abuse and a misfortune for the human race.

Some theologians teach that in Paradise the cold *mine* and *thine* will not exist. They thereby attribute the legal basis for property to the failings and weaknesses of fallen human nature. Now failings cannot be the legal basis, and above all, they cannot be the basis for a natural right.

This objection obviously rests on a misunderstanding. Such theologians regard the failings and weaknesses of human nature indeed as a basis why the institution of private property is necessary, but by no means as a legal basis for it. It may very well happen that something emerges under certain conditions as a necessary means to preserve the natural order, which under other conditions would perhaps not have been necessary. And so, such theologians also indicate that for people, as they actually are today, private property is indispensable for the proper development of individual and social life, whereas they assume that before original sin, the division of goods would not have been called for.[1] —

Some of the Fathers of the Church, it is further objected, seem to trace private property back solely to unjust force. Thus, for example, we find St. Ambrose (I,1 *de offic.* c. 28): *Natura omnibus in commune profudit.....usurpatio* [2] *vero fecit privatum.* And St. Basil said: (*Homil. in Luc.* 12,18): *Si quis loco in theatro ad spectaculum occupato deinde ingredientes arceat, id sui ipsius proprium ratus, quod ad omnium communem usum proponitur, tales eiusmodi quoque divites sunt. Nam communia praeoccupantes ea ob praeoccupationem sibi assumunt.*

The Fathers of the Church in their time fought against absolute private ownership and hard-hearted riches. Against that they emphasized that goods are not here for the preservation of individuals, but they are destined for all people; and in this sense, they are by nature common to all. Goods came to be owned by individuals only by a positive state of affairs; and this state of affairs took on to some extent the nature of an act of violence, a theft, if the rich seized everything for themselves in unbounded greed, and forgot the obligations that are implied by property ownership. —

The point of view was also ascribed to St. Thomas Aquinas that private property owed its origin, even as a social institution, solely to positive human law. That is incorrect. Indeed, Thomas taught[3] that the *distinctio possessionum secundum humanum condictum* was *quod pertinet ad ius positivum, ut supra dictum est* (q. 57, a. 2 *et* 3). If then in q.57 I. c. he ascribed it to the *ius gentium*, then this *ius gentium* is in any case, according to the one explanation, not the same as *ius naturae,* and also not the necessary consequence of a provision of the *ius naturae,* but a legal provision stemming from human freedom. The other statements of St. Thomas (which we deal with later) allow no doubt, however, about whether the Angelic Doctor takes the *distinctio possessionum* to be an obligation as established in the natural law, whereas only the way it is carried out follows positive law. — According to another explanation, St. Thomas understood *ius naturale* only as being the directly evident principle of law, whereas he regards the *ius gentium* as the conclusions arising of necessity from those highest principles; and they therefore also enjoy virtually universal recognition among all nations. Thus, St. Thomas regards, for example, the statement, "You should honor contracts" and "Thou shalt not steal" as belonging to the *ius naturale* in the present as well as in the Aristotelian sense. The Angelic Doctor therefore does not deny, but, in fact, affirms the natural law basis of property, inasmuch as he ascribes the same to the *ius gentium*.[4]

Max Maurenbrecher too[5] admits that in their judgment of such teachings of Aquinas,

"the Catholic scholars came much closer to the truth than their Evangelical opponents. For, actually there are passages where Thomas includes the property right, even if not under the 'law of nature' in the strict sense of the word, nevertheless under the 'natural law.' We have seen...that he divided this 'natural law' into two parts, of which the one includes what is in itself natural, and the other includes what is a natural law condition by certain consequences.[6] The former he calls the 'natural law' in the narrower sense, and the latter, 'the law of nations.' The former is common to all living beings, and the latter only to all people; the former rests on what are innate, more instinctive impulses, the latter is a product of the 'natural law' as Aristotle used the word,[7] as opposed to positive law. Now it is on this 'natural law' that Thomas based also private property. The 'natural law' in the narrower sense to be sure has nothing to do with it; for, in itself, there is no reason why, for example, an acre of ground should belong to this person and not to another: 'in itself all things are common,' as he said at another point.[8] But for certain consequences....it is nevertheless 'natural' that the acre of land has a particular owner; and therefore the right to ownership belongs to that second part of the 'natural law,' the 'law of nations.' Now that corresponds entirely to the view that private property is a fulfillment of the 'natural law' in the narrower sense of the word, because the 'law of nations' is precisely the actual 'law of reason.'

The passage on which Maurenbrecher refers here (*Com, in Eth.* V. *lect.* 12b) reads:

The natural law is that to which nature prompts the person. But now we may distinguish a twofold nature in man: an animal one, which he has in common with the animals, and a human one, which is peculiar to him as a person, i.e., insofar as he distinguishes by his reason what is disgraceful and what is honorable. However, the jurists regard as the natural law only that which stems from an impulse of nature, which is common to men and the animals, like the bond of a man to a woman, the raising of children, etc. However,that kind of law which also stems from actual human nature, insofar as man is reasonable, the jurists call *ius gentium,* because it is in use among all nations, e.g., that we must honor contacts, etc.

Thus, it is clear how fallacious the assertion was that Thomas believed in an original communism, or that he recognized this, and not private property, as a natural institution.[9]

Socialist writers or agitators like to appeal to the example of the first Christians and to monasteries as favoring communism.

But today, there is no longer any doubt according to the testimony of the best authors[10]

that among the first Christians there was no real communism. Also in the community at Jerusalem there can at no time be any question that there was real communism, but only of a highly developed kind of care for the poor (the organization of distribution), which came so close to the ideal, that no one suffered any want, and every rich person treated his possessions as the property of all. The reason that this condition actually appeared to be like a community of goods was due to various circumstances: 1. the full fraternal charity by which all members of the community, rich and poor, accepted each other, the basis for the great generosity. *Rev.* 4: 32 introduced the way in which the poor were provided for with the reference, that all 'were of one heart and one soul;' 2. these Christians lived in closest ties with one another in virtually a family-style relationship, from which it turned out that actually, and so far as use was concerned, no one any longer regarded his personal property as his own possession. That is why *Revelations* 2:44 indicated: 'All who believed were together and held all things in common.' Paul saw himself inclined time and again to have collections in his communities (1 *Cor.* 16, 1,3. 2 *Cor.* 8; 9,1. *Romans* 15, 26). Indeed, in the contract which the so-called Council of Jerusalem concluded with Paul about the division of their missionary work, it was proposed that the Apostle to the Gentiles, in order to recall at all times his continuing relationship with the Jewish mother Church, should always remember the poor of Jerusalem (*Gal.* 2:10). Thus, care for the poor must have been a constant and heavy burden for the leaders of this community. — If we sum it all up, then we can explain the communistically inclined tendencies of the *Acts of the Apostles.* The fact that these actually wanted to say nothing more than that care for the poor was taken care of in full measure, is clear from 41:34: *Neque enim quisquam egens erat inter illos,* which is presented as the result of an alleged communism of goods. These words, however, contain a very definite reference to *Deuteronomy* 41:34: *Et omnino indigens et mendicus non erit inter vos.* The Old Testament prescription presented therein about practical love of neighbor reaches its pinnacle in this statement. The *Acts of the Apostles* wishes to show by adopting those words that among Christians the complete fulfillment of that Old Testament prescription was achieved; but it does not have communism in view anymore than Moses. Furthermore we can see from the *Acts* that individuals, and especially outstanding members of the community, did own private property. In 12:12, there is reference to the house of Mary, the mother of John Mark. It was in Christian ownership; for here the faithful were assembled during the time of persecution; and it was here that Peter turned after he was freed, as to a secure place of refuge.[11]

More recent socialists admit that in the first Christian communities there was in fact no common ownership of the means of production, but only a communism of use and consumption, especially with regard to food.[12] However, the community was no more the legal subject of the ownership of consumer goods, than it was of the means of production. A comparison of the relevant texts[13] proves conclusively that all sharing was traced to the obligations of Christian charity. A man should share, but "each one, as he has determined in his heart, not grudgingly or by compulsion; for God loves a cheerful giver."[14]

And now the communism of the monasteries! First of all, it is based on a free decision by each individual, and on a freely elected sacrifice of personal independence and ownership, out of higher motives. Furthermore, it presupposes a continuing self discipline, a domination of all natural instincts and inclinations, a persevering spirit of sacrifice, a high moral capacity for self-denial, of which the great mass of humanity is incapable. The whole world or an entire nation will not permit itself to be turned into a religious community. Such selflessness, as is required in religious life, will instead be found always and everywhere only in a smaller circle, with a relatively small number of persons, to whom God extended the extraordinary grace of a vocation to this state in life.[15]

3. On the assumption that private ownership, especially of land and soil exists, there will of necessity arise a great disparity with regard to the material condition that exists among people. But that contradicts the *natural equality* of people.

It is an ancient, often refuted fallacy from which this objection stems.

If I talk about "the human person" in general and in the abstract, about man as a being endowed with essential characteristics of being composed of body and soul which go along exclusively with the human person, then it is true that people are all equal; because abstract "humanity," being a person, or the essence of man, is present in all. However, where do we find this person in the abstract?[16] If we observe man as he actually exists, in the concrete, in his individuality, and if we compare ages talents, bodily strength, we see everywhere a significant inequality.

And what needs to be noted is an inequality which comes from nature; for it is nature which makes individuals, as it does the species. Indeed, to state it more pointedly, nature constitutes the individuals, and man derives his species from them. The conclusion is therefore entirely correct that all human individuals are by nature unequal among themselves to the extent that we look at their individuality, just as they are equal from nature as to their species.

The inequality in possessions therefore corresponds to the *natural, individual inequality* among people. Liberatore also noted very incisively:[17]

Private property (especially in land and the soil) brings with it inequality among people, in the same way as industry, trade, and every activity undertaken with an application of insight and energy bring with them. He who works more, who is more ingenious, who knows best how to help himself, gains more. And by gaining more he can, if he is moderate, honest, and wise, accumulate more savings and provide himself with wealth which becomes the source of new riches.... So what is to be done? Should we out of love for equality do away with thrift, ambition, moderation, and moral integrity? What is most typical is that the defenders of equality at the same time praise freedom. And they do not grasp the fact that liberty and equality contend with each other. Two living beings could not keep themselves equal for even one day. By the fact that they are free, their actions would be different; and these would lead to differences in the emergent results, whether we are talking on the level of morality, or law, or economics.

If we talk about "inequality" which stems from ownership, then we eventually envision, as a rule, a condition where enormous accumulations of wealth stand opposed to total destitution. That kind of inequality which arises from bad social conditions, is not what we are speaking of here.

But that does not apply to inequality as such. That is not only not a bad condition, but a benefit for society. If some were not richer in temporal goods than others, and therefore in their tendency to have greater wants and inability to fulfill them, so as to be more dependent on the services of others, and if others were not poorer in temporal possessions and happier with bodily and, above all, also with spiritual strength, then social life and genuine unity among people would hardly be conceivable. This need for help, however, which applies to all, and especially to the greatest and richest, is a warning to them that despite all external differences they are essentially equal, and that they depend on one another, that they are all obliged to reach out for the reciprocal benefit of the whole of society. That is the principle of *solidarity* on which society is established by God. Each person is tied to every other person, and the community itself must answer for all of its members.[18]

4. If we designate the institution of private property as a social necessity, then social democracy sees it as *the root cause of all social evils*. Greed, envy, waste, avarice, luxury, exploitation, theft: all of that would have to cease if we would once do away with private property.

Is it really still possible to doubt that without private property, the temptations to crime would still abound? Even envy, avarice and greed would very certainly not disappear from the world with the abolition of private property. Anyone who has an inclination to these vices and who does not fight against them from inside himself, will also not be rid of them under the dominion of communism. He will be stingy with the satisfaction of his wants, and he will quietly pile up what he has gained by this niggardliness. He will seek to appropriate from common ownership as much as he can; and even if he cannot use it, he can nevertheless possess it. That is, of course, the very nature of avarice, such a person does not derive pleasure from the use of goods, but from having them. So crime will not cease, not even the crimes of property, and even less so, crimes of other sorts.

Certainly private ownership may provide the motivation for many crimes and vices; but the root of this lies not in the property, but in the vices of human nature. Many a good institution is spoiled by the fault of people. The same holds for private property. In itself, as a right, property is something that is very good for man, and it is indispensable for society. But the free human person can make evil use of a right that is in itself beneficial, in such away that a curse instead of a blessing attaches itself to the institution of private property. That is precisely our situation today. There has been lacking for a long time, and there is undoubtedly still lacking, an adequate legislative protective barrier against the abuse of property and of the power inherent in it. But as we do not kill a sick person in order to heal him, so also we cannot abolish the institution, private property, simply because all that is lacking is a structure of property ownership which is in conformity with the general welfare.[19]

¹Rodbertus-Jagetzow (cf. *Zur Beleuchtung der socialen Frage* [Berlin 1875] p. 222), in opposition to Christian philosophy, recognizes no necessary connection between human nature and private ownership of the means of production, but who sees instead in the ownership of land and capital only a transitory, purely historical phase of economic development. — Even Rodbertus talks about at least a *relative* necessity of property, i.e., of a necessity "for the present time." He says, "I do not believe that the free will of society is strong enough today to already make unnecessary the motivation to work which that institution (ownership of land and capital) still provides.... I do not believe that society has completed its journey through the wilderness, that its moral vigor is already adequate in order to be able to affirm and and attain the promised land of redemption from the ownership of land and capital by free labor." — We too, along with certain of the Fathers of the Church, do not believe in an absolute necessity of private ownership. Yet the promised land, where the cold *mine* and *thine* does not play any role, where work itself provides nothing but joy and pleasure, free of all thorns, — is according to Christian doctrine a paradise that was long ago lost by original sin, whereas Rodbertus awaits it in the future. No, human nature will not change no matter in what direction historical evolution may move. It will continue with all of its advantages, but also with all of the handicaps of its fallen condition, as it is today, — in need of redemption, partaking in guilt and punishment, but having forfeited forever the diadem of original justice as that existed in Paradise. — Cf. Schiffini l.c.p. 173ff. — Thus, private property is *de iure naturae hypothetico*, i.e., the natural law calls for it as a prerequisite of the present fallen condition of mankind.

² The word *usurpatio,* which St. Ambrose used, is generally used in the Latin language also for *legitimate* occupation. Cf. Cathrein, *Moralphilosophie* II, Bk. 4, § 5, 3rd ed.) 312ff.

³2,2,q.66,a.2 ad 1.

⁴Cf. St. Thomas, 1,2,q.95,a.2. — Also the other Scholastics have acknowledged *necessity* or a necessity-like quality of private property, even if they had differing opinions about the manner and form in which distribution took place. Thus, for example, Molina (*De iustitia et iure* I, tract. 1, disp. 4, n. 8) and Suarez (*De legibus lib.* 2, c. 14, n. 13; c. 17ff.) believed that one could not explain the original distribution of goods without the intervention of positive law or of a contract. At the same time, however, they admit that human nature, and therefore the natural law, called for some distribution. Thus, they by no means contested the natural law basis of private property. (Cf. L. Molina, *de iustitia et iure* I, *tract. 2,* disp. 20. — *Fr. Suarez, De opere sex dierum* I. 5, c.7, n. 17). Cf. Lehmkuhl, *Theologia moralis* I, n. 906. Cf. Cathrein, *Moralphilosophie* Pt. I, Bk. 9, §2 (3rd ed.), 497ff., Pt. II, Sec. 1, Bk. 4, §5 (3rd ed.), 315ff.

⁵*Thomas Aquinas Stellung zum Wirtschaftsleben seiner Zeit* (Leipzig 1898) p. 113. 117. — Cf. also Franz Schaub, *Die Eigenthumslehre nach Thomas von Aquin und der moderne Socialismus* (Freiburg 1898) p. 259ff.

⁶S. Thomas, 2,2,q.57, a. 3c.

⁷Cf. *Com. in Eth.* V, *lect.* 12b.

⁸Cf. *De sortibus* c. 2. S. Th. 2,2,q.66, a.2 *ad* 2.

[9]The false interpretation which Prof. Albert Ritschl imputes to St. Thomas (*Festrede zur Feier des 150 jährigen Bestehens der Universität Göttingen* 1887) was rejected by Prof. v. Hertling (*Zur Beantwortung der Göttinger Jubiläumsrede* [Münster and Paderborn 1887] p. 9ff. Cf. also Hertling, *Kleine Schriften zur Zeitgeschichte und Politik* [Freiburg 1897] p. 135ff.). Also Luthardt, Gottschick, and Wendt find intimations of communism in Thomas. Other Protestants, on the other hand, like H. Ritter, H. Contzen, Jhering, Ashley, Lippert, and then as we saw, Max Maurenbrecher, declare the followers of Aquinas to be free of communistic tendencies. — Cf. also from Catholic literature: Franz Walter, *Das Eigenthum nach der Lehre des Hl. Thomas und des Socialismus* (Freiburg 1895). - Franz Schaub, *Die Eigenthumslehre nach Thomas von Aquin und dem modernen Socialismus* (Freiburg 1898).

[10]Cf. Dr. Georg Adler, *Geschichte des Socialismus und Kommunismus.* Leipzig 1899. (*Frankensteinisches Hand- und Lehrbuch der Staatswissenschaft.* Pt. 1, vol. III, p. 69ff. — Ratzinger also deals with this question thoroughly, *Geschichte der kirchlichen Armenpflege.* 2nd ed. 1st ed. (1868) p. 15f.

[11]*Kölner Korrespondenz für die geistl. Präsides.* publ. by Dr. P. Oberdörffer. 6th yr. (1893) p. 163f.

[12]Cf. Bernstein and Kautsky, *Geschichte des Socialismus* I, 26f.

[13]*Romans* 12:10; 13:20. 1st Cor. 6: 1ff.; 7:30; 11:20. 2nd *Cor.* 8:3; 9:7. !st *Thess.* 4:6. 9ff.; 2nd *Thess.* 3:8, 10:12. *Eph.* 4:28. 32. 1st *Tim.* 6:17f.

[14]Cf. A. Winterstein, *Die christliche Lehre vom Erdengut* (Mainz 1898) p. 116ff. 136ff.

[15]Cf. Card. de Lugo, *De iustitia et iure* d. 6, n. 1. After de Lugo explained the social necessity of private property, he continued: "*Cum tamen hoc stat, quod in aliqua bonorum congregatione utile sit ad pacem, nihil proprium habere singulos, ubi nimirum propter singulorum perfectionem et animorum concordiam haec omnia inconvenientia facile vitantur, deputatis aliquibus, qui res communes administrent et singulis necessaria provideant, prout fit in coetibus religiosis. In tanta vero hominum multitudine modus ille vivendi utilis non esset, quia perfectio apud paucos reperitur.*"

[16]Taparelli 1. c.n. 355.

[17]*Grundsätze der Volkswirtschaft* (German: Innsbruck 1891), p. 196f.

[18]Rev. A. M. Weiss, O. Pr., *Sociale Frage und sociale Ordnung oder Institutionen der Gesesllschaftslehre* II (3rd ed. Freiburg 1896) 618.

[19]Cf. Theodor Meyer S. J., *Institutiones iuris naturalis* I, n. 475.

Chapter 6

OBJECTIONS TO THE NATURAL LAW BASIS OF PRIVATE PROPERTY

1. For the American social reformer, Henry George,[1] it is not simply private ownership of the means of production, but specifically private ownership of land and the soil which is the real cause of the progressive concentration of ownership on the one hand, and of the ever-increasing impoverishment on the other. Small wonder then that the encyclical of Leo XIII, *On the Condition of Labor* , found little sympathy with Henry George. In an *Open Letter to His Holiness Pope Leo XIII,* [2] he sought to dissuade the head of the Church from the natural law basis for private ownership as expressed there.

Addressing the Holy Father, George said:

> You say 'that what is purchased with rightful property is rightful property.[3] However, purchase and sale alone cannot confer a right to ownership, but only transfer it. Ownership which has in itself no moral justification is in no way able to confer that justification by the fact that it is transferred from the seller to the buyer.[4]

How grateful the Pope must have been for such learned instruction as, for example, that whoever buys stolen goods from a thief, does not acquire ownership of what he has purchased! The Pope obviously knows what all moralists and jurists teach unanimously, that in a case of derivative acquisition, only that can be acquired which the one who transfers it actually and rightly owned. *Nemo dat, quod non habet.* Also, unknown to Leo XIII are the principles and provisions of Canon Law about the *bona fide* — the good faith of the possessor — principles which carry over fully to all other legislation. Otherwise, how could he have clearly and forthrightly assert: "That which is purchased with what is legitimate ownership, is legitimate ownership"? So long as I myself did not steal the money with which I purchased the stolen goods, then I acquire "legitimate" ownership of the purchased object.

The matter is immediately clear, if we look at the position that is contested by George in its context. The Pope is complaining about the difficult conditions of the present era. However, he rejects the cure which the socialists imagine that they have found in the common ownership of goods. As his first argument against the socialistic plans, Leo XIII warns that it will be precisely the working classes that will be severely hurt by it. The Pope defends this position as follows:

> It is surely undeniable that, when a man engages in remunerative labor, the very reason and motive of his work is to obtain property, and to hold it as his own private possession. If one man hires out to another his strength or his industry, he does this for the purpose of receiving in return what is necessary for food and living; he thereby expressly proposes to acquire a full and real right, not only to the remuneration, but also to the disposal of that remuneration as he sees fit. Thus, if he lives sparingly, saves money, and invests his savings in land for greater security, the land in such a case is only his wages in another form. Consequently, a working man's little estate thus purchased should be as completely at his own disposal as the wages he receives for his labor. But it is precisely in this power of disposal that ownership consists, whether the property be land or movable goods. The socialists, therefore, in endeavoring to transfer the possessions of individuals to the community, strike at the interests of every wage earner, for they deprive him of the liberty of disposing of his wages, and thus of all hope and possibility of increasing his stock and of bettering his conditions of life.

That is to say, the Pope is by no means presuming here, as George assumes, the justification of private ownership of land and the soil from the mere fact of the purchase; but presupposing that, he designates it as a right of the worker to use his wage for acquiring by purchase a parcel of land. The proof for the justice of private ownership in general, and of land and the soil in particular, is developed elsewhere by the Pope.

Yet it was already a foregone conclusion for George that a justifiable private ownership of land and the soil was impossible, and that it could not therefore be acquired by a purchase Entrapped by this prejudice, he even believed that according to the basic idea of the papal encyclical, the acquisition of ownership of slaves could be justified just as well as the acquisition of ownership of the land. George stated:

> To verify that if we have only to substitute for the word 'land' the word 'slave' in our argumentation. Then his statement would read as follows: 'It is surely undeniable that, when a man engages in remunerative labor, the very reason and motive for his work is to obtain property, and to hold it as his own private possession. If one man hires out to another his strength or his industry, he does this for the purpose of receiving in return what is necessary for food and livelihood. Thus, if he lives sparingly, saves money, and invests his savings, for greater security, in 'a slave', the 'slave' in such a case is only his wages in another form; and consequently, a working man's little estate thus purchased should be completely at his own disposal

like the wages he receives for his labor.[5]

What naivete! If land and the soil could no more become private ownership than the slave, then the travesty which George imputes to the words of the encyclical would have some sense and purpose. But it must rank as of some importance that the slave is a human person, and that man, as such, cannot be the object of a material right, as is fully applicable in the case of a thing. George, on the other hand, places slavery and land ownership on the same level. For him they are merely two different forms of one and the same "robbery," twin measures by which the corrupted human sense make it possible for the strong or the shrewd to circumvent God's law about work, inasmuch as he compels other to work for him.

> Does it make a difference whether I own only the land on which another person must live, or if I own the man himself as property? Am I not just as much his master in the one case as in the other? Can I not force him to work for me? Can I not take as much of the fruits of his labor as his activity makes possible? Do I not have the power of life and death over him? For to take from a person the land and the soil, is killing him, as much as if I take his lifeblood from his veins, or as if I deprive him of air by putting a rope around his neck. [6]

Actually, it makes a whole lot of difference whether I only own the land or if I regard the person himself as my property. In the latter case, the person becomes for me a thing which is totally surrendered to my arbitrary discretion. In the former case there is a person who works on my land, as a contracting party, as a free being, not only of his very nature, but also freely in fact and in practice. So long one single person does not own all land by himself, and so long as in society not every person who does not call any part of the land his own must work as a farm worker, the possibility remains open to him to change masters, and to function in one or the other branch of production. Thus, I can "force" no one to work for me. Nor do I hold, by my ownership of land, the power of life or death. For, in a well-organized society which is governed by just laws, it will neither be permissible for the land owner to do as he pleases with the land and the necessary products for satisfying the wants of the members of society, nor to charge a price which is not commensurate with the value of the products, nor, finally, to withhold the just wage from the workers employed on his land. —

2. The papal encyclical asserts: "The origin of private ownership of land is human reason." In opposition to this, George acknowledges that reason and foresight are attributes of man, which elevate him above the animal and impress on him the mark of divinity. He also does not contest that this gift of reason leads to the need for a right to private ownership of anything which can be made available

by reason and foresight, as well as what can be provided by physical work:

> The right of private ownership exists undeniably in all things for which
> *human* reason and foresight have provided. However, it cannot apply to
> the elements for which we have to thank the reason and the providence of
> God.[7]

If, by that, George had only intended to say that in his relationship to God,
man ranks not as the owner but only as the responsible administrator, we would not
have to refute him. However, the American agrarian communist does not admit of
private ownership of land for man. For him, property is not a social institution
meant to govern the relationship of people to the material world within the life and
business of society, but the theft of something that is given by God, and intended
not for a few, but for all.

> To explain that further, let us suppose that a society wanders through a
> desert, as the Israelites came out of Egypt. Those among them who had the
> foresight to provide themselves with containers of water would have a
> legitimate right of ownership over the water that they had brought along
> with them in that manner; and in the middle of the parched desert those who
> are thirsty, who failed to take advantage of the opportunity, could ask for
> water from the others as a favor, but not as a right. Even though the water
> as such is owed to the Providence of God, its presence in jugs and in that
> area was made possible only by the foresight of a few people who brought
> it with them: therefore these have an exclusive right to it. But let us assume
> that others had hurried ahead with the intention of taking possession of the
> wells in the oases as their own property, and that they would allow those
> who come later to drink water only in return for payment. Could this kind
> of foresight bestow a right of ownership?

If we wish to be nasty, we could ask those who follow George to show us the
essential difference that exists between the "work" of "running ahead" in the desert,
and carrying water. However, we do not wish to obscure the point of the assertion.
According to George, the water in the well is a free gift of God for all people. But
as soon as someone takes that from its natural container and carries it into the
desert, it turns into the legitimate property of individuals because the individual
"produces" the water again by changing its location. In the desert, the water that has
been transferred there is not a mere gift of God, but a "product of human labor."
Now one should be humane enough to not expect of us that we first carry every
drink of water into the Sahara so that we can enjoy it as our property. If we
understand George correctly, it is already enough to have drawn the water from the
well in order to rank as its "producer."

But what kind of comparison is this? What idea does it express? According to
George, productive labor by a person is the only legitimate title to ownership,

whereby "productive" is taken in the broadest sense, including simply a change of location. Therefore there can be no property aside from the product of human labor. That is the basic idea on which all other conclusions rest — the leading notion to which George time and again returns. George himself formulates this idea as follows:

> People who stand as individual beings with individual wishes and capacities are personally justified in using their talents and to enjoy the full product of their activity. From that emerges the right to own the kinds of things which are created by labor; a right which derives its validity from the natural laws, and which is older than the laws of human beings; a right to property which the owner may transfer; but to take the right from him, that is — theft.

Up to this point, we agree with George completely. However, he goes further when he asserts: "This right to property which stems from the right of the individual to his person, is the only fully valid right to property; it applies to all goods produced by labor, but it cannot also apply to the elements which God has created.[8]

George's approach is obviously erroneous, just as it also does not grasp in its full depth and extent the dignity and power of the dominion of man over the material world. To his thesis, we juxtapose another: What is wrought by human labor is not the only legitimate title to property because this title itself in turn already necessarily presupposes another and higher legitimate title.

a) According to a universally recognized philosophical principle, being precedes action. If therefore a general legitimate title to private ownership already follows from a man's being, then this legitimate title must undoubtedly precede every other legitimate title associated with the action of man. Now, however, the existence of man already in fact indicates, his personality, his self-awareness, his freedom, the status of being in charge of the whole world as God conferred this when he gave him the possession of this earth, while at the same time bestowing on it qualities which correspond to human needs, and furthermore, the natural necessity and obligation according to which man must use external goods to preserve his existence, to develop his capacities, and to achieve his goal. — All of this announces in a satisfactory manner the right of the lord of creation which precedes every productive activity, to appropriate the goods supplied by the earth, which he needs. Therefore the "right of the human being to his personality," of which George speaks, i.e., the right to the capacities and the fruits of his activity, may in fact constitute a universal, abstract legal basis for establishing the necessity of private ownership as an institution. But it is by no means the ultimate and deepest legitimate title. Man has the right, as a *human being,* to acquire private property, before he can lay claim to it for himself as a *producer.*

b) For if he did not have the right as a *person,* he also would not have it as a producer. Why? Henry George was keen enough to appreciate that wherever the validity of the right derived from production stands opposed to an older right to some specific thing, work cannot rate as a legitimate and acquisitive title. Otherwise every kind of theft would be a title to acquisition, since the thief removes a movable thing from the custody of someone else, so that he is at least a "producer" by changing the location of the thing. Since all things are the property of God, so man could not acquire any material good as the "fruit of his labor," if it is not the God-ordained purpose of the creatures to serve man, and if man had not received this dominion from God himself, by virtue of which he could supply himself with material goods for his purposes, and had thereby received in advance the right to appropriate things. Thus, also the right to the fruits of the engagement of personal energies cannot be the only and ultimate legitimate title to private property, because to have validity it necessarily presupposes another, higher one derived from the divine will, from the personal existence of man, and from human existence and nature.

Moreover, our deduction by no means denies the universal obligation to work. Even the deepest and ultimate legitimate title to private property does not exclude the necessity for work. To actually apply the right of dominion, and therefore the first affirmation of a material right to a specific thing, work is always required, at least the work of first taking possession. However, the mere naked fact of work taken by itself does not alone create ownership, but work insofar as it is the way or the means to exercise a personal right: whether it is the right of dominion of people over the external world, or whether it is the right of dominion over one's own capacities, and their actions and fruits.

c) George acknowledges the property right with regard to all goods produced by work. He denies it with regard to the original goods which God has created — the natural endowments which were created without human work. In order to not immediately trap himself in a contradiction, he expands the concept of "productive" labor so that it includes also simply taking something into one's possession. "If someone catches a fish in the ocean, he then has a property right to the fish."[9] If someone draws water from the well, he acquires a property right to the water. Why? Because the water now finds itself in a container by human work, and because the person has brought about a change in its location.[10] However, this expansion of the concept of "productive" work does very little for Mr. George; instead, it demonstrates precisely the untenability of his position. For it is obvious that in the aforementioned cases, man simply brought about a change of location, whereas ownership extends precisely to the substance of the fish and of the water. If accordingly we, as people, did not have a right to appropriate "gifts of nature," then there would not be any question at all about ownership.

George recognized the force of this objection very well. But he sought to remove himself from it in a manner which did not exactly do credit to his intelligence. Let us look at what he himself said:

> It would be worth our while to refute those people who say at this point, if private ownership of land is unjust, then private ownership of the products of labor is also unjust, because the original material for all products likewise comes from the land. Furthermore, it will appear on closer observation that all human production is analogous to bearing arms. If a person plants grain, melts metal, builds houses, weaves material, or engages in any kind of productive activity, he is basically doing nothing other than changing the location and the form of goods which are already present. As the producer, man is merely the one who changes the form of a thing, not its creator. God alone creates. Now since the changing of form, which is actually what production by people amounts to, becomes a part of the material so long as the form lasts, then the right to private ownership fuses together the form with the material; and it thereby confers also a right to own the natural material in which productive work has embodied itself.[11]

Entirely correct. But that obviously applies on the assumption that man can actually acquire ownership of a gift of nature or God which he did not create himself — an assumption which the theory, that ownership is only permissible for goods produced by man, flatly contradicts. One may assume that George read the encyclical *Rerum Novarum* carefully. But that makes it all the more remarkable how it could escape him that Leo XIII used a similar pattern of thought as he himself uses in order to prove with convincing force precisely the private ownership of land which George opposes. In the encyclical we find:

> Now, when man thus spends the industry of his mind and the strength of his body in procuring the fruits of nature, by that act he makes his own that portion of nature's field which he cultivates — that portion on which he leaves, as it were, the impress of his own personality; and it cannot but be just that he should possess that portion as his own, and should have a right to keep it without molestation.[12]

And shortly after that the Pope says:

> For the soil which is tilled and cultivated with toil and skill utterly changes its condition; it was wild before, it is now fruitful; it was barren, and now it brings forth in abundance. That which has thus altered and improved it becomes so truly part of itself as to be in a great measure indistinguishable, inseparable from it. Is it just that the fruit of a man's sweat and labor should be enjoyed by another? As effects follow their

cause, so it is just and right that the results of labor should belong to him who has labored.

Therefore, so long as it cannot be contested that the cultivation and improvement of the land is the "product" of labor that is created by man, it will also be impossible to allot to man only the fruits of the land improvement. Rather, we must assign this itself to him, and thereby acknowledge in principle private ownership of land and the soil. That is in fact a consequence of the proposition which George establishes when he says: "Since the transformation from which the production by man actually arises fuses itself with the material, so long as the form persists, the right to private ownership fuses the form with the material and thereby bestows also the right to own the material of nature in which productive labor has embodied itself."[13] Because cultivation stays with the soil, so the right of private ownership fuses the "form" with the "material," and it thereby confers also the right to own the soil in which productive labor has embodied itself.

Yet George tries anew to withdraw himself from this conclusion inasmuch as he makes a distinction between the natural material which is contained in the human products, and the land itself:

> Even if man can take the material from the supply house of nature and change its location or form as he pleases, from the moment in which it is taken from it the material seeks to return again to the supply house. Wood decays, iron rusts, stones erode, whereas among the transient products, some survive for a few months, others only for a few days, and yet others immediately disappear as they are used. Despite the fact that, so far as we can see, material is eternal and the energy lasts forever, and despite the fact that we can neither destroy nor create even the smallest atom in the sun's rays, so also every human work which moves or binds together disappears in the necessary changes in nature. Thus, the recognition of a property right in original material which is embodied in products of human labor never signifies more than temporary possession, and it never subtracts from the supply that is intended for all..... Therefore we heartily agree with you, when you say: human reason gives the individual a right, to permanently possess things that are for consumption, but also the right to the long term and future uses of certain goods. You are right insofar as you include such goods as buildings which can outlast the human lifetime, along with food articles or firewood which are immediately used up. But when you conclude from this that man can enjoy a right of private ownership of natural elements which are present from all eternity and which will last for eternity, goods on which all are dependent, then you are definitely wrong. Man may well enjoy a right of private ownership of fruits of the earth derived by his labor, since these will in time lose the form which they derived from labor, and they will return to the supply house of nature whence they came, and because the right to own such goods does not harm anyone; but he cannot own the earth itself in that way, For it is the great supply house from which are taken not only the material for production without which man cannot accomplish

anything, but from which also their own physical subsistence derives.[14]

George brought up a truth of the greatest significance when he says that man may not appropriate the soil of the earth like a thing that is destroyed by first use, e.g., the piece of bread which man consumes. In fact, as Leo XIII emphasizes, the earth is a "storehouse that shall never fail,"[15] from which all must derive their livelihood. But it was not good that George used this truth, which was so important for social reform and for economic policy, to cover the vulnerable position into which he undeniably put himself. For, his assertion moved in the direction that man could only acquire private ownership of what was produced by him. But when we draw his attention to the fact that every kind of ownership is contradicted by this theory — the material, the substance of all so-called products was a gift of nature, was created by God and not by man — he becomes evasive. He says: "wood rots, iron rusts, stones erode." That substance, that natural material, does not remain in ownership for long, whereas the earth, of its nature, does not draw a precise time limit on the property right. However, that is an entirely different question than the one being contested. Or cannot the duration of ownership be one that is limited by the nature of the object owned, while true ownership of such an object can nevertheless persist? George confuses the right and the duration of ownership. Therefore his proof is refuted. Even if the golden treasures of our millionaires revert to "the great storehouse of nature," what would follow from that? Obviously only one thing: that no property lasts for ever, but not that there can be no right to own natural material.

3. George's attacks on the papal encyclical have thus far had little success. Perhaps another reservation is of greater importance:

> Your own statement that the land and the soil are the inexhaustible supply house which God provides to man, must have evoked an uncomfortable reservation with your Holiness with regard to its appropriation as private property. For, as if you wanted to put yourself at ease, you assert further that the ownership right of individuals must not harm the rights of others. You say: the earth does not cease to satisfy the needs of all, even if it is distributed into private properties, because those who have no land receive the products of the land in payment for their labor. Assume that someone poses the following question to your Holiness as a judge of morality: 'I am one of several brothers to whom our father has bequeathed a parcel of land which is sufficient to sustain us. Now since he did not designate any parcel of these for any of us in particular, and since he left the division to us, I as the oldest took the entire piece of land for myself. Yet, by doing so I did not deprive my brothers of their sustenance; for I allowed them to work on my land, and out of the products paid them a wage equal to what I would have had to pay other laborers.' How would you respond? Would you not tell him that he has committed a mortal sin, and

that his excuse enhances his crime? Would you not order him to provide restitution to his brothers and impose a penance on him?[16]

Undoubtedly the Pope would decide precisely in that way. And the reason for the decision is clear. For, if the father of a family as the testator did not undertake to make a division of his estate among his children, e.g., he did not assign this to A, and that to B as their individual parcels of land, then the children would nevertheless, as soon as the estate is turned over to them, at the moment of the testator's death, already acquire a right to a particular and, indeed, equal portion of this distinct, specific estate. If the oldest takes the entire estate as his own property, he robs his siblings of their well-established right, and he therefore makes himself guilty of a sin, and he burdens himself with an obligation to make restitution. Now it is something quite different when the father of a family leaves an estate to his children, and when God, the lord of all men confers the right to derive his sustenance from the goods of this earth by work. The difference may be traced to two factors.

a) The general assignment of the human race to the possession of the earth does not confer to the individual person either a direct claim to some specific thing, nor a legal claim to a certain quota of natural endowments. It constitutes the highest legal basis for private ownership *in abstracto,* but not its legal title *in concreto.* In other words, by virtue of that assignment man has the right to acquire property, but he does not get an established property right to some particular, specific thing or quota of things, nor the custodianship of a particular object or of a particular quota. The Holy Father presented this truth in a clear manner that could scarcely be misunderstood, when he said:

> And to say that God has given the earth for the use and enjoyment of the universal human race, is not to deny that there can be private property. For God has granted the earth to mankind in general; not in the sense that all without distinction can deal with it as they please, but rather that no part of it has been assigned to any one in particular, and that the limits of private possession have been left to be fixed by man's own industry and the laws of individual peoples.[17]

This means that it is in particular the industry of a man and his work — and it involves the legal institutions of peoples which are to determine and regulate the subsequent acquisition of ownership to any particular things. It is otherwise in the case of inheritance. The children of the testator not only have the right to acquire something. In addition, they have an already established right to some quantitative, even if not specific, portion *in individuo* to a quota of this actual inheritance. The inheritance claim, or the right to inherit what is intestate, is not an abstract basis for them, but it is already a concrete legal title which confers on them a legal claim to ownership of the estate, indeed, according to their share of it. Add to that:

b) an essential difference between the equal entitlement among the children who have a claim to the father's estate, and the equal rights of people to get goods from the universal storehouse of nature. George says: [18] "As equal creatures of the Almighty, who have equal rights to live out their lives under His providence and to satisfy their needs, people also have equal rights in the use of the land and the soil." If George had understood that "equal right to the use and enjoyment of the land and the soil," as it is to be understood — as an abstract entitlement following the specific equal nature, but differing in its concrete established content, just as also the individual nature of people emerges in great variety — then his words would truly have been full of wisdom. But then it would have been impossible for him to sustain the parallel between the inheritance right of children and the right of people to enjoy the goods of the earth. Or could we assume now that it remained hidden to him, that the children destined to share an inheritance have not only an equal right, but beyond that, a right to a claim to the same — to the equal share as their own? But no, he by no means overlooked this circumstance. Instead, the assumption that God assigned to each person in the same way to acquire ownership left him unsatisfied. He wants to assert precisely that from nature, by virtue of the Divine will, everyone as a child of God has the right to an "equal share"[19] in the enjoyment of the earth's goods — an assertion which he appears to apply significantly only to the land and the soil. Therefore, along with the older and more recent land ownership reformers, he wants to "nationalize" the land, i.e., to turn over all ownership of it to the state. In this way he hopes to be able to assure to all the right to the land and the soil, whereas at the same time he does not want to put anything in the way of the continuance of private ownership of land, and indeed differing private ownership according to various titles.

However, it appears to us that George contradicts himself by his assertion that all people, as equal creatures, are also fully equal in their right to the actual use of land and the soil. He requires that "the equal sharing in the advantages of the natural resources of our divine Father should be assured to all people in equal portion."[20] Now we cannot understand at all how he can limit the "equal claim" of all people to the "land and the soil of the fatherland."[21] George perhaps knew the Principality Lippe-Detmold. The "fatherland," Lippe-Detmold, is very exiguous; and if we assume that there, or in the Free Hansa City of Hamburg, all may lay claim to an equal share in the land and soil of the fatherland, then the share of each individual will in any case be much smaller than the share of the occupants of a larger country with a less sparse population. Now what happens to that equality of which George talks, and which he calls for because we people are all the equally beloved children of the divine Father? What happens to equality if this heavenly Father assigned to his children only a part of Lippe-Detmold, whereas to others he assigned far greater forest and land areas in Brazil or in Africa? How does one reconcile that with the adduced theory that "all people" — that is also the people of Lippe-Detmold — "have to be assured the same share in the advantages of the natural treasures by our divine Father"? And what about the assertion that in the distribution of the earth's surface the same principle applies as "where a human father leaves his property in equal portions to a number of children?" [22]

Henry George was certainly keen enough to realize that a common ownership by all of humanity of the land and the soil is full of theoretical and practical absurdities. Precisely for that reason he put in the place of humanity the individual nation, the tribe, the state. However, it also should not have remained a mystery to him that by doing so he contradicted his own basic principles. For if the individual, as opposed to humanity — i.e., the sum total of children of the heavenly Father with equal rights — perpetrates an injustice by the fact that he acquires a portion of the land as private property, then also the state and the nation will fail in entirely the same manner inasmuch as they regard a particular territory as their own, to the exclusion of other nations.[23] Thus, either common ownership by all of humanity over all of the earth — or private ownership by individual persons of portions of the earth! There is lacking any basic support for the collective ownership by a nation of its territory, to the exclusion of other nations.

4. However, Henry George sees in the private ownership of land not only a violation of the equal rights of people, but also a total exclusion of the non-owners from the common inheritance. Pope Leo XIII establishes the opposing point of view:

> Moreover, the earth, though divided among private owners, ceases to thereby minister to the needs of all; for there is no one who does not live on what the land brings forth. Those who do not possess the soil contribute their labor; so that it may be truly said that all human subsistence is derived either from labor on one's own land, or from some laborious industry which is paid either in the produce of the land itself or in that which is exchanged for what the land brings forth. [24]

Mr. George's displeasure with these words appears to have been significant. It shows in the somewhat undignified manner in which he formulates his opposing view:

> Assume that Your Holiness served as a temporal prince over a land that has no rain, like Egypt, where there are neither wells nor brooks, and which is

provided with water by a remarkable river like the Nile. Assume that you have sent out a number of your subjects to cultivate the land, and you wished them success and suggested that they treat each other justly. Soon, however, you would be informed that some have laid claim to ownership of the river, and that they withheld from the others every drop of water which they do not buy from them, so that the owners of the river became rich without work in this manner, whereas the others were impoverished despite their hard work because of the high payments for water, so they could barely stay alive. Would you not be highly indignant? Assume that the river owners would then send to you the following excuse: 'Distributed as always among the individuals, the river does not cease to serve the entire community; for no one is thirsting who drinks the water of the river. Those who do not own river water have their work by which to acquire it, so that one may say: all water is either taken from one's own river, or it is derived from work in some other branch of industry which is either paid for with water or in something else with which one can purchase water.' Would the indignation of your Holiness be any less? Would it not become even greater because of the insult to your intelligence contained in this excuse? I do not have to point out to your Holiness more clearly that between the absolute denial of God's gifts to a person, and denying it to him in a way other than by purchase, there is a difference as between a robber who allows his victim to die, and the robber who requires ransom money for his life.[25]

The thought process of George is very smooth. Too bad that it has to be refuted as flawed. It suffers:

a) from a false approach to primary occupation, the mode in which it is carried out, and the duration of its effect. If we are to believe George, then there would only be a few persons who, hurrying ahead of others, would occupy the whole earth for themselves and leave the hindmost to all the rest. And he liked to express this, his approach, at times in a very dramatic manner: "When Cain and Abel were the only people on earth, they were free to divide the earth among themselves."[26] We will not even call to mind that Cain and Abel were never alone on the earth. It is enough to establish that George considered the division of the earth between two people as possible. That corresponds entirely to the approach which already previously lay at the basis of the examples produced by him:

Does the guest who appeared first have the right to deny the occupation of all chairs, or to demand that no one partakes of the meal who will not agree to the requirements which he prescribed? Does the first one to present an admission ticket at the door of the theater and who enters it have the right to close the doors since he came first, and to enjoy the presentation all by himself?[27]

Here there are not even two; it is just one who lays claim to everything. Cathrein[28] already made us aware that Cicero,[29] and Thomas Aquinas[30] had long since laid such objections to rest. One who shows up first at the theater does not have the authority to exclude all others. But he does have the right to choose a seat and to exclude all others from his seat. The same applies with regard to taking possession of the earth. He who comes first can choose a place for himself to establish his residence. He may fence in his field, build his house, and call both his own. Those who come after him may do the same. However, they do not have the right to rob the one who came first of his property. In fact, not one or two persons, but people in indeterminate numbers can acquire land ownership Even today the point in time is still far off when vast stretches of Africa, Asia, and Australia will be fully divided up.

The source of the error which George fell victim to is, in our opinion, the false assumption that by the purely intrinsic fact of a simple act of the will, or by one's oral announcement, occupation could be fully accomplished. Therefore he assumes that Abel and Cain were able to divide the whole world between themselves, and that they could set forth for all newcomers how they could enjoy the fruits of the earth. If this assumption were correct, there would be nothing in the way of even taking possession of the moon, and their lordships the judges would already have been presented with disputes to decide who among several persons first had the *animus possidendi* with regard to the lunar landscape. Yet, George's assumption is a flawed one. Two factors are required to acquire something by occupation. *Adipiscimur possessionem corpore et animo.* The mere will is not enough. There must be added the externally recognizable condition of actual occupation, the *animus possidendi* must be embodied in some way in the external conditions. Therefore it was physically impossible for Abel and Cain to divide the whole world among themselves, because only a part of the earth was available for them to work on , and only a part was attainable by them.

As was the case regarding the manner and form of occupation, so George also erred with regard to the duration of the right which stemmed from it. One who reads George's presentation will be inclined to believe that the same persons who accomplished the first occupation still sit today on their plot of land, armed to the teeth, in order to maintain their "theft" against "people who were born later." However, that hardly conforms to reality. Death comes to everyone, and with it the confiscation of all goods which they owned until then. The "people who are born after them," to the extent that they are physical heirs, or if they are perhaps put into the will as heirs, move into the position of the testator whose property right is erased with his life. However, the legitimate title which the following generation gets to the land is no longer occupation, but its own hereditary right. Therefore George's reservations are invalid, where he says:

Is the temporal priority of occupation supposed to provide an exclusive, eternal title to the surface of the earth, which uncounted generations are supposed to observe according to natural succession? Does the earliest generation therefore have a better right to this earth than we? Or than persons one hundred years ago, or than those a thousand years ago?[31]

George need not worry about that! He has the same right to acquire ownership, as long as he lives, as those do. However, death will also knock at his door. He cannot exclude the coming generations "forever" from the house in which he lives. Other generations enjoy the same rights after his property rights are extinguished. —

Then it must appear to us therefore:

b) that for George there is a totally false approach to the relationship between landowners and the rest of the members of society, as also about the nature of society where there is division of labor. In a society with division of labor not all citizens can and will busy themselves with cultivating the land. Some carry on this, others another, kind of business. If the businesspeople are dependent on the farmers who provide nourishment for their bodies, so the farmer is dependent on industry, on crafts, on commerce, without which many of his wants would not find satisfaction. He who has money in his pocket is neither a slave nor a tribute payer to the landowner. If the farmer produces more corn than he can eat himself, then he is so dependent on the rest of the citizens that, without the patronage of the consumers, he cannot even cover his own costs of production. We are quite willing to admit that a person who owns land and soil is, in a certain sense, in a better situation than the person who has no such property. However, the love which God has for all people also has not prevented Him from providing to one and the other person those talents and opportunities so that scarcely a person is endowed with the same natural capacities, and he finds himself in the same good situation. In any case it is scarcely in accordance with objective circumstances when the examples selected by George always designate the landowners as people who hurried ahead of the others in order to occupy a "river," or a "well" which flows constantly. In our present situation, does our farmer sit with the ladle in hand ready to provide a cooling drink from the barrel of nature to anyone who pays the "land rent?" Nature remains niggardly, and its productive forces must as a rule be activated by the sweat of the farmer. "The earth is the mother, labor is the father," Petty said; and he was right about that. At any rate George intended to indicate most clearly with the examples he chose that in the price of the product a "rent" was also included for the natural fertility of the soil — a rent which rises as population density increases, since the price of the product and, with it, also the price of the land increases. Yet, his examples suffer from such great exaggeration that one would be tempted to believe he read his theories in the stars, and that he did not draw them from the observation of human labor.

We have only to look at the world as it is in reality, and we have only to go to Germany or to Italy in order to recognize that, here as there, it is precisely the farmer still occupying his "own" plot, who has often become a person who pays tribute to mobile capital. Interest which the landowner has to pay to capital is often greater than the rent which the farmer derives for himself from the fertility of his acreage. This is what we would like to direct the attention of all reformers to, and we recommend that they study this matter. Then we will no longer see the millionaire capitalists standing at the door of the peasant's hut, starving and begging for a drink of water, pleading for some corn and wheat to quell their hunger, whereas at the same time with tears in their eyes they present the "tribute" which the thieving farmer has imposed on them. Instead we would recognize that capitalistic liberalism is the enemy of the wealth of nations, and as it fattens up on *usura vorax* it deprives the farmer of his fields, robs his homestead on which the parents dwelt and the children derived their nutrition with honor. We will recognize that it is not the ownership of land, but the abuse of property, which is guilty of the land speculation that is detrimental to the common good, and of so much that hastens the ruin of nations. This abuse is responsible for the depredation of the once fertile Campanga, the depopulation and enervation of Italy, which cleared the way for the Goths and the Vandals, and which delivered Roman Britain to the worshipers of Odin and Thor. It is not private ownership which was responsible for the fact that in the once rich and populous provinces of the East the thinning ranks of the legions were destroyed by the curved swords of the Moslem hordes, and that the cross which stood on the Holy Sepulcher and also on the Church of St. Sophia was pulled down, to be replaced by the half moon. It was not private ownership which turned the fertile fields of Scotland over to the wild beasts for their habitation, and which changed them into pasture for cattle in Ireland, and led to the land lying fallow in England and in Australia. We cannot accuse private property of all of these sad facts which were so damaging to the common good of nations. The owners of property are the guilty ones; — that greed which, according to the words of the prophets, drives people to amass fields as if they were the only ones on earth — that flawed system of private property which runs counter to the rights of the whole community, and which in some places made private ownership of land a private monopoly for a few — liberalism with its free enterprise. — Those are the enemies who could enrich their devoted partisans by the sweat of the peoples' blood, until the nations finally mustered up the courage to break the oppressive chains.

Also, George confused the institution of private property with the way it was put into operation, because he proceeded from the false assumption that there is only one kind of property, absolute property, only one single order of property, that which surrendered to the owner the unrestricted free use of his goods. So long as he acknowledges ownership of the fruits of labor, he calls this right an "unrestricted one except in such cases where the obligation of self-preservation abolishes all other rights."[32]

5. The other objections which George raises against the reasoning in the papal encyclical present little that is new, and they are refuted sufficiently in what has been said here. Thus, for example, George rejects the assertion of the Pope that "the labor expended on the land gives an ownership right to the land itself."[33]

The meaning of the words of the Holy Father has already been presented by us previously. Leo XIII does not say that labor, by the mere fact that it is labor, confers a right to own the soil. Generally, in order for a fact to provide a title for concrete acquisition, it must be traceable to a legal basis which involves the right to acquire ownership very generally. Only insofar as, and to the extent that a concrete, specific fact is subsumed under this general and absolute legal basis does it become a legitimate title to acquisition in the individual case. Now the universal legal basis for getting ownership of material things is also the property right which the person has by virtue of of his activities and their fruits. However it is not the ultimate, most universal, and highest legal basis, but instead it necessarily presupposes as a higher legal basis the consignment to man of this world and the right provided by God to make the earth serve him. — Nor does the Pope assert that every kind of work applied to the land confers a property right to it. For the Holy Father does recognize the wage relationship where a worker who is in the employ of another person does not acquire ownership of the product as his right. According to the other assumption, work would even lead to its own undoing, since every person could come along and rob private property inasmuch as he had only to use it as the object of his work. What the Pope is talking about, according to his unambiguous language — as George also accepts[34] — is only the original acquisition of ownership of a piece of land which until then belonged to no one. But here labor is in fact the legitimate title to acquiring ownership. Otherwise the first cultivator of the land could not call the fruit of his labor his own. For, what is the fruit of his labor? The wheat which grows on the field that was made fertile? Undoubtedly; but that is the indirect fruit. The direct effect of his cultivating labor, its immediate "fruit," is the improvement on the land itself, the improved land. Indeed, so far as its substance is concerned, the land is no more created by man than the coat which the tailor finishes. However, the form of the cultivated soil was acquired by it only through human labor, and this form cannot be separated from the land any more than it can by itself be the object of ownership. The confused state in which George found himself with regard to this argumentation led him to add other objections one after another, without ever coming to terms with the weakness of the particular ones by doing so:

1) Granted that work justifies also the original acquisition of ownership of the land and the soil, still it would not be in a position to justify the private ownership of land "as it exists in our time."[35] However, the Pope is not talking about present-day property and the individual present-day owners. He is developing the natural law basis of private ownership in general. If someone wants to challenge the legitimate titles of individual private owners, Leo XIII would not stand in his way if he overthrows those which had "their origin in force and deception."[36]

2) George asks: if the work performed confers the right of ownership of land and the soil, then where would the limits of this property right be; and for example, does this property right remain valid as soon as it becomes clear that the land has rich mines, etc.?[37] But what does this imply? — It is enough that the natural law approach, of necessity, leads to the assumption of property on the surface of the earth. All further questions can be left to positive, legislative provisions. Roman law allows ownership of the land and the soil to extend to the unmeasured depths and heights. German law, on the other hand, treats minerals and the like as treasures of nature, and it assumes that they are unowned so long as no possession of them took place by mining. The right of occupation was already limited in olden times to the ownership of the surface of the earth. On private parcels of land, private parties could plant; on the common march, the associates of the march could do so, and on unowned land, anyone could. Later on, the state took over the right of occupation as a mining royalty for itself. In more recent times the mining royalty has again been done away with, but mining is limited by special rules in the public interest. Thus, as this example shows, viewpoints and approaches about "the limits of the ownership right" can change even within the confines of the same country, without the legitimacy of private land ownership being questioned in any way. —

3) It makes little impact then, when George argues in the following manner: "The labor expended on land and the soil provides the right to own only the fruit of the effort, but not the land itself, just as work on the ocean confers a right to the ownership of the fish, but not a right to own the ocean."[38] In the same way he had already made visionary observations about how, if someone plants grain, "he acquired a right by doing so to own the grain which he harvests; but he can make no similar claim to own the sun which brought it to fruition, nor to the earth on which it grew."[39] Truly remarkable! Since when is the sun cultivated by people like

the land? And since when did the ocean take on a new form by fishing, as did the land which man cultivated? The sun is too far out of our reach. Here any actual possession and therefore also any ownership is impossible for people. Indeed we could burn our fingers if we attempted to occupy this powerful ball of fire. And to take possession of the ocean is meaningless. Fishing in particular would not become more remunerative by people appropriating the ocean,[40] whereas the need for a more intensive cultivation of the land has always been associated with its private ownership.

4) It arouses George's indignation that those who own the land benefit without further ado from the increases in value which arise as a consequence of the growth of population and by improvements made by the state or the community, public improvements, etc. We are content to recall in this regard that neither does a population increase trace itself back to the work of the state or of the local community, nor can the increase in land value, specifically in the cities, be designated in the true sense of the word as the "product" of a population increase. It is a consequence of the greater density of population, as it represents also a consequence, but not a product brought about by improvements made by the state or the local community. However, George's own theory allows to someone the property right only to an actual and immediate product — to what he "created." By what right, then, does he attribute to the state or the local community any value increases, any new values which are in no way the product of work by the state or local community? And is he really trying to establish the proposition: everything which benefits another following from my own action, becomes my property? Then one day an American private company which erects a magnificent public building near our houses, e.g., a station, could lay claim to the value increase in the parcels of property, by the same right as George was prepared to assign value increases to the state which were brought about by state or local community projects. —

6. But George is not finished yet. He denies the assertion by the Pope "that private ownership of the land and the soil is approved by *public opinion,* and that it has been conducive to peace and tranquility, and that it has been sanctioned by a divine commandment."[41]

Thus, first of all, private land ownership is not supposed to be approved by public opinion: "Even if it were true that public opinion accepts the private ownership of land, this would not more establish justice than the once universal acknowledgement of slavery made that right"[42] Nevertheless, if private ownership of land were something that applied only to one single period, or to one or the other era, like slavery, then the objection of George would be justified. However, Leo XIII relies on the public opinion not of one era, but of all times and all nations which have shared in the growing development of civilization and culture. But when George refers, in response, to the "original" communism of all peoples, and when he asserts about property ownership: "It came into this modern world by your forefathers the Romans, whose civilization it corrupted and whose empire it destroyed,"[43] he is making use of a position which in our time has already been scientifically refuted.

Among the many reasons in favor of private property, Leo XIII also includes the one that mankind "has consecrated by the practice of all ages the principle of private ownership, as being preeminently in conformity with human nature, and as conducing in the most unmistakable manner to the peace and tranquility of human life."[44] This remark directs itself first of all only against communistic and socialistic systems in the strict sense of the word. However, against them the indicated proof is of decisive validity. By it the Pope is not denying that some systems could be conceived where, at least in appearance, provision could be made for order and peace as is the case in a society based on private ownership. What he is asserting is simply the obvious fact that mankind has for centuries seen in private property a natural basic condition for peaceful living conditions.

It is quite unusual when George permits himself to lecture the Pope on exegesis.

> Your Holiness indicates that a commandment of God sanctions the right of private ownership of land, inasmuch as you present the following passage from Deuteronomy: 'You should not covet your neighbor's wife. You should not covet your neighbor's house or field, nor his male or female slave, nor his ox or ass, nor anything that belongs to him.' If your Holiness is suggesting that the word 'field' here implies a sanctioning of private land ownership as it exists today, then we should conclude with even greater justification that the words 'male or female slave' signify here a sanctioning of human slavery; for it is clear from other passages of the same book that these expressions refer as well to the contemporary serfs as well as to slavery. But here the word, 'field' refers to the concept of use and improvement of the land to which a right of occupation and ownership applies, without acknowledging a right to own the land itself. That this reference to the field cannot amount to a sanction of private land ownership as it exists today, is proven by an additional passage in the Mosaic Book of Laws which expressly denies the right to own as unjust and unfit. Jehovah says, 'The land shall not be sold in perpetuity; for the land is mine, and you are but aliens who have become my tenants.' And it is prescribed accordingly that the land should revert every 50 years to the original owners or to their heirs, whereby, in the simple conditions of making a living at that time it was supposed to make it impossible to permanently assign a man his place on God's earth.[45]

Let us begin with the last! It is not true that Jehovah's word denied as unjust and unfit the right to own land. At any rate, the earth appears as a free gift of God to man, as a country "which the Lord, your God gave to you." But does this mean that man cannot lay claim to any right to own, as opposed to another person, if he appears even in his relationship to his God only as a renter or an administrator? Do not precisely the commandments of the Mosaic Law, the provision that every 50 years the land should revert to the original owner or to his heirs — establish a very stable ownership which should not be taken from its rightful owners by indebtedness? Furthermore, where in all the world is it written that the state has to lease land to the members of society? Or does George somehow identify the state with Jehovah, and derive the state's ownership from Jehovah's all-embracing dominion? The earth belongs to me, says Jehovah, — not: to the state. "I" lease it, — not the state. Therefore, how can George pretend to find support for his theory in Holy Scripture?

Just as absurd, finally, is George's assertion that the commandment: "You should not covet your neighbor's wife. You should not covet your neighbor's house or field, nor his male or female slave, nor his ox or ass, nor anything that belongs to him," could only be appealed to in order to protect the ownership of the field, if we likewise take it to imply approval of the ownership of the servant and the maid. Indeed, why not also as a justification of the ownership of the wife? The commandment seeks to protect the right of the neighbor himself against covetousness. Whether this right is the right to property or not, the commandment as such says nothing; and it uses instead the general expression "nor anything that belongs to him." The ox and the ass, just like the field, were then entirely private property; and also this private property is protected by the divine law. —

7. George goes on to tell the Pope,

> You say furthermore that the fathers are supposed to provide for their children, and that private ownership of land is necessary for that, so as to make possible such providence....[46] Therefore Your Holiness believes that it is an obligation of fathers to leave useful property behind for their children which is supposed to preserve them from poverty and misery in the fortunes of this temporal life.[47]

Let us compare this with the words of Leo XIII:

> In choosing a state of life, it is indisputable that all are at full liberty either to follow the counsel of Jesus Christ as to virginity, or to enter into the bonds of marriage. No human law can abolish the natural and primitive right of marriage, or in any way limit the chief and principal purpose of marriage, ordained by God's authority from the beginning. 'Increase and multiply.' Thus we have the family; the 'society' of a man's own household; a society limited indeed in numbers, but a true 'society,' anterior

to every kind of State or nation, with rights and duties of its own, totally independent of the commonwealth.

That right of property, therefore, which has been proved to belong naturally to individual persons must also belong to a man in his capacity of head of a family; nay, such a person must possess this right so much the more clearly in proportion as his position multiplies his duties.

For it is a most sacred law of nature that a father must provide food and all necessaries for those whom he has begotten; and, similarly nature dictates that a man's children, who carry on, as it were, and continue his own personality, should be provided by him with all that is needful to enable them honorably to keep themselves from want and misery in the uncertainties of this mortal life. Now, in no other way can a father effect this except by the ownership of profitable property which he can transmit to his children by inheritance. [48]

The Pope is affirming three things here:

1) The father of the family has, as such, the right to acquire and to own private property;

2) He has the obligation to support his children and to provide such care to them (*ut victu omnique cultu tueatur, quos ipse procreavit*).

3) Furthermore, nature leads him (*a natura ipsa deducitur*), to wish (*ut velit*), to acquire that whereby his children may be made secure in the face of temporal uncertainties. But he can only accomplish that by the ownershiop of productive things (*fructuosarum rerum possessione*). Then even in the face of sickness and the like, when children may be prevented from doing physical or mental work, they are protected by ownership and will not have to depend on the alms of others or on the state.

Does all of this imply that every individual father has the obligation to leave behind parcels of land for his children? For, who has nothing, can leave nothing behind. Some will leave capital to their children, and others, parcels of land. Perhaps most fathers must limit themselves to do nothing more for their children than to assure them a good education. However, this does not deny that the wish and effort of fathers to leave behind property for their children is entirely legitimate and natural, and that a social order which makes such a hereditary transfer impossible by abolishing property would come into conflict with the natural and the legitimate desire of a father's heart. Therefore it is entirely without substance when George proposes to the Pope: "The obligation of the father toward his child can only be an obligation that is possible for all fathers."[49] Leo XIII does not require that every father leave behind land, but only that every father provides for the future of his children according to his own situation. —

8. George objects further: "You are also of the opinion that the right to private ownership of land motivates people to lead productive lives, increases wealth,

settles people down, and bolsters the feeling for the homeland."[50] That there is in private ownership a powerful incentive to lead a productive life, George does not wish to contest. He passes over this point in silence, and he is satisfied to point out that in his system too there is no lack of incentives. Indeed, George sees the main motive to cultivate the land intensively as being in the security that one can harvest the fruits of one's labor, the results of one's work. This assurance, however, he feels is adequately provided to the extent that the cultivator of the land is guaranteed only a continuing right to occupy, without ownership. "In the crude stage of human society, where all activity limits itself to hunting, fishing, and picking wild fruits, private ownership of land is not necessary. However, as soon as people begin to cultivate the soil, and when they apply their effort to lasting work on the soil, then private possession of the land becomes necessary in order to assure the property right over ownership of the products of one's labor. For, who would want to sow without being assured of the exclusive possession of the land, which is necessary for the harvest? Who would undertake to install costly structures without the exclusive right to the cultivated land, as would alone make it possible for him to derive the benefits of his work and of his capital investment?[51] However, George proposes that the assurance of deriving the fruits, which stems from private occupancy would be enough; indeed it is greater than exists in today's tenancy system.[52] —

We do not want to contest whether the assurance of the tenant will be greater if the owner of the land is not a private person, but the state. We are content with the tacit admission that it is at least less than the assurance which the present-day private owner of the land has. And Dr. Eugene Jäger says rightly that,

> In fact, if the land ownership reformers believe they can get by with simply leasing the land,[53] so that the state would in some way derive only the land rents, and that these at the same time would be the sole taxes (single tax), whereas the whole surplus value remains in the hands of the private operators, then they will soon go wrong with their social reform just as the social democrats with their communistic arrangement of production and consumption. The tenant who is not sure whether he and his heirs can retain ownership of the land (a decree by the government, a 'law' could in fact rob him of such private ownership) will hardly be inclined to invest labor and capital into the land to a significant degree, so as to strive for the surpluses in production whose further useful and lasting realization would be made practically impossible for him. Here too an atrophy of economic intensity must soon appear.[54]

When Henry George decries the unnatural and miserable, barbaric housing conditions in the large cities, and when he points with justifiable indignation to the fact that countless people have no home in their fatherland, and when he recalls, in particular for present-day Italy, the words of Tiberius Gracchus: "Romans! People acknowledge you as the lords of the world, and still you have no right to a foot of your own soil! Wild animals have their holes, but the warriors of Italy have only water and air!" — then these complaints certainly find a most sympathetic response in the heart of Leo XIII. But it is not property as such, but the manifold abuse which is responsible for that misery, an abuse which is by no means intrinsically connected with the institution of private property, an abuse which can be done away with least of all by taking away from all their own home in the fatherland.

9. Also the final objection which George raises against the presentation of Leo XIII only brings to light new misunderstandings: "Finally, you are still of the opinion that the right to own land and the soil privately is a natural one and that it does not come from man; the state has no right to abolish it; taking the value of the land away by a tax would be unjust and horrendous against private property owners."[55]

It appears to us that George did not know what we understand by a "natural right." Otherwise it would be hard for him to oppose the natural law basis of private land ownership in a new separate context, after he had already disputed previously that "the origin of private ownership of land is human reason."

The natural law comes from God as the highest Lawgiver. However, the herald of this lawgiver, the manifesting principle of the natural law, is human reason. So if private ownership of land contradicts human reason, then it also goes counter to the natural law of God. On the other hand, if it appears as a requirement of human reason, as Leo XIII points out in a convincing manner, then the attempt to do away with it would at the same time involve a violation of the natural law and the order intended by God for man and for human society. The natural law, as reason manifests it, contains solely the universal legal bases for private property, but it does not of itself confer the particular legal claims *in concreto*. In other words: the natural law teaches the justification and necessity of private ownership as a institution, and along with that the right of man to acquire property according to this or the other juridical and morally admissible manner. However, the natural law does not of itself establish the concrete relationship of a particular thing to some individual person. It leaves that instead to the activity of people. And yet, precisely that seems to be George's approach to the "natural law" basis of private property. Or would he otherwise have been able to pen the following words:

> Who would dare to trace the personal right to own land to a direct wish by the Creator of the earth? In what manner does nature confer that kind of property right? Does it acknowledge it in some way? Can any one ascertain by a difference in growth, in the face, in the build or color of skin,

by dissecting their corpse, or by an analysis of their strengths and needs, that one person is predestined to be a land owner, and another is by his nature destined to be a tenant?[56]

At any rate, physiology, chemistry, or anatomy provide no legal claim to ownership. The designation of the individual owner is accomplished in another manner, by his own action, his work, his derivation of the fruits, etc. And the fact that these things *in concreto* establish a right to the ownership of this thing for this person — that is also indicated by reason, by the natural law, which clothes such facts with its legal operation. —

10. Just one word in conclusion. George believed that the state has the authority to abolish private ownership of the land, since it was the state that introduced it. And he is unhappy with the Pope because he now presents an opposing view. That is all the more remarkable since George had already approved previously any absolutism as destroyed in the proclamation by the Pope.[57] We have in mind the words of the encyclical: "Man is older than the State and he holds the right of providing for the life of his body prior to the formation of any State." [58] If man is older than the state, what right has the state to steal those original rights of individuals and families? Was it somehow established for this purpose? Did people unite themselves into political communities so that things would be worse for them than previously? Or is it not precisely one of the essential tasks of the state to protect the temporally and logically prior rights of citizens? On what title should the ownership of land by the state base itself? Would it therefore not appear to be a unique act of violence if the state somehow, as George proposed, took away by a single confiscatory tax the "entire value of the right of land ownership in favor of the national community"?[59] We readily admit that the progressive concentration of land ownership in the *latifundia* countries was not accomplished, as it is not now being accomplished, without "robbery" in the narrow and broader sense of the word. But all of that is still child's play, compared with the grandiose "robbery" which George was so bold as to propose. —

We have perhaps discussed George at greater length than his sociopolitical importance merits. However, it was not the social reformer George who claimed our attention, but the critic of the papal encyclical *Rerum Novarum* and the opponent of the natural law basis of private ownership of land. Furthermore, George ranks as the keenest and most clever of the modern agrarian socialists; and it is for that reason that his objections rated greater attention.

¹Henry George regarded the social problem not as a production problem, but as a distribution problem, so much so, in fact, that his socialistic land rent theory culminated in the proposition: "The abolition of the private ownership of land must be accomplished by expropriation or confiscation of land rents." By this principle George hoped to be in the position to eliminate social misery from the world, and in that way he set himself apart from the social democratic theorists of the old world. Henry George who reached an age of only 58 (he was born on 2 September 1839 in Philadelphia, and he died on 30 October 1897), led a very eventful life. He began as a book printer, and then he became a gold seeker in California, worked as a typesetter in various newspaper offices in San Francisco, traveled to India and finally wrote for the *San Francisco Times* anonymous articles which aroused much attention. Their authorship scarcely became known when the owner of the paper made him the editor and soon afterwards the chief editor of this paper. Yet, he gave up his position in 1867 in order to edit in turn the *Herald*, and then the *Evening Post*. In between he was the gas inspector and the head librarian in San Francisco, traveled about Great Britain where he was under police surveillance for a time as a "suspicious individual," studied working conditions there and at home, and finally established in 1887 in New York, where he settled down, the weekly *Standard*, in which he first set forth his unique social political theories. What drew the most attention and made him known in broad circles were this two works, *Progress and Poverty*, and *Social Problems*, of which the first German translation went through five editions, and the second one, three.

²*Zur Erlösung aus socialer Noth* (The Condition of Labour). German by B. Eulenstein. Berlin 1893.

³Cf. Encyclical *Rerum Novarum* para. 4.

⁴*Offener Brief*, p. 22.

⁵*Ibid.* p. 22.

⁶*Ibid.* p. 23.

⁷*Ibid.* p. 25

⁸*Ibid.* p. 2f.

⁹*Ibid.* p. 3.

¹⁰*Ibid.* p. 26.

¹¹*Ibid.* p. 26.

¹²*Rerum Novarum* para. 7.

¹³*Offener Brief*, p. 26.

¹⁴*Ibid.* p. 26f.

¹⁵*Rerum Novarum* para. 6.

¹⁶*Offener Brief* p. 28f.

¹⁷*Rerum Novarum* para. 7.

¹⁸*Offener Brief* p. 2.

¹⁹*Offener Brief* p. 4.

²⁰*Ibid.* 20.

²¹*Ibid.* p. 6.

²²*Ibid.* p. 4.

[23]Cf. R. J. Holaind S. J., *Ownership and Natural Right* (Baltimore and New York 1877) p. 87f.: "Either land belongs to the whole species, or it does not; if the former be true, then we can have no exclusive ownership: exclusive ownership of a nation makes the wrong *national* instead of *individual* ; that's all. If it does not belong to the whole race collectively, then any one not debarred by preexisting rights can appropriate. There is no foundation whatever for the exclusive ownership of a nation, as separated either from the collective ownership of the race, or the individual ownership of the citizen. If one has not the right to appropriate land, how many will it take to make a full-fledged right? Would not their collective ownership look very much like an addition of zeros?"

[24]*Rerum Novarum* para. 7.

[25]*Offener Brief* p. 29f.

[26]*Ibid.* p. 4 f.

[27]*Progress and Poverty* p. 247f.

[28]Vol. 5, of the first book of *Die Sociale Frage* (Freiburg 1892). 3rd ed. 1896.

[29]*De finibus* c. 20.

[30]*S. theol.* 2,2,q.66,a.2.ad 2.

[31]Cf. *Progress and Poverty* p. 247. Cathrein *op. cit.* p. 66.

[32]*Offener Brief* p. 4.

[33]*Ibid.* p. 31.

[34]*Ibid.* p. 31.

[35]*Ibid.* p. 31.

[36]*Ibid.* p. 31.

[37]*Ibid.* p. 32.

[38]*Ibid.* p. 32.

[39]*Ibid.* p. 3.

[40]Cf. W. Roscher, *Grundlagen der Nationalökonomie* I, 87.

[41]*Offener Brief,* p. 35.

[42]*Ibid.*

[43]*Ibid.* p. 36.

[44]*Rerum Novarum* para. 8.

[45]*Offener Brief* p. 39.

[46]*Ibid.* p. 39.

[47]*Ibid.* p. 40.

[48]*Rerum Novarum* par. 9-10.

[49]*Offener Brief* p. 42.

[50]*Ibid.* p. 44.

[51]*Ibid.* p. 4.

[52]*Ibid.* p. 44.

[53]It does not matter that George wanted the service of the landowner to the state to be known not as "rental interest," but as a tax.The relationship between the state and the private owner nevertheless remains analogous to a rental one.

[54]*Denkschrift über die Lage der Landwirtschaft für den VI Ausschluss der Kammer der Abgeordneten. Beilage 373 zu den Verhandlungen der Kammer der Abgeordeneten,* II (Munich 1894), 1292.

[55] *Offener Brief* p. 45.
[56] *Offener Brief* p. 46.
[57] *Ibid.* p. 7.
[58] *Rerum Novarum* para. 6.
[59] *Offener Brief* ; p. 47.

Chapter 7

THE ACQUISITION OF PROPERTY

1. Our discussion up to this point dealt with the origin and the natural law foundations of the institution of private property in general.

There remains the question: in what way does ownership arise in specific cases, i.e., the ownership of an actual thing by a physical or moral person? How is the right of property over some particular thing acquired for someone or by someone?

By nature every person has the right to acquire and to own property. That follows from our proofs of the necessity and the justification of the institution, private property. For every person has from nature the undeniable right to preserve his life, to make reasonable provision for the future, and to fulfill himself. And everyone has the right to establish a family and to provide for it on a continuing basis. Finally, every person has the right to enjoy the fruits of his industry, whether these fruits are the physical products of work, or the wage for work performed in the service of someone else.

Now nature itself did not confer the actual ownership of certain specific objects to anyone — not to the individual person; who wishes to state that A owns that house, and B owns that field directly from nature? Not even all of mankind in the collective sense. For if that kind of positive and actual collective ownership stemmed from nature, then the individual would always be dependent in the acquisition and use of goods on the will and the approval of all other people as being the original co-owners. But now it is impossible for a right which stems directly from nature, as that is found fully and entirely, and emanates in every individual person, to be entirely dependent on the arbitrary will of another person. And so the assumption of a natural, positive, collective ownership contradicts reason as much as it does the most ancient sources of history.[1]

2. But if nature did not confer on anyone any actual property, then it is proper for me to say: in the nature of things everything is common to all, but:

First: it is common not in the positive, but in the negative sense, because goods do not belong to anyone actually, but to all potentially. They are *res nullius,* and neither an individual person nor all of humanity has the right to exclude anyone from its acquisition and use.[2] The kind of goods which were *res nullius* belonged to this so-called "negative community of goods" and they still do so today.

Second: it is not common in the collective sense, as if all people together, like the members of a society, had a communal potential or actual ownership of the goods of this earth,[3] — but in the distributive sense, since each individual has from nature not an actual, but still a potential right to own, i.e., the right to acquire goods. From nature, the individual goods do not belong to one person more so than to another; and therefore they can be acquired by the one or the other, or even by many together. The acquisition of actual ownership of a thing is therefore disjunctive.

3. Since nature does not confer on anyone the actual right of ownership of any one specific thing, some actual human factor is required by whose mediation the ownership of a specific individual thing will be acquired, whether by one individual person, or by a community of persons.

The objection is raised against this, that a mere fact cannot possibly establish a right, and in addition, a right which abolishes the potential property right of all other persons to the thing in question. It is precisely on this basis that Pufendorf felt he could not dispense with the assumption of a consensus of all other people for the legitimate establishment of ownership.[4] However, he overlooked that it is not the fact by itself which established a concrete right of ownership, but the fact in association with a legal provision from which it derives its juridical force. Without that kind of legal title to acquisition, there is no legitimate acquisition, i.e., acquisition based on a right.

4. For two factors belong to a so-called "legal title," to acquire ownership: a general *legal provision,* and a *fact,* by which that legal provision is applied to a specific case.

Thus, for example, the following universal principle would be a legal provision: "Each individual who has acquired a thing for himself by legitimate purchase or gift, has the right to ownership of this thing." On the assumption of the legitimacy and the juridical effectiveness of that universal principle, a specific person would now obviously have to be recognized as the owner of a concrete thing, insofar as the person could simply prove the fact of the gift or the purchase.

Cathrein says,[5] "One could therefore view the legal authority as at least a kind of deduction drawn from a syllogism, whose major premise is a general legal provision, and whose minor is a particular concrete fact:"

Anyone who duly purchases an object, acquires ownership of it. (Legal provision).

But now A has duly purchased that object. (Fact).
Therefore he is the owner of it. (Legal authority).

The legal provision by itself, or in association with the fact, is in truth the actual *titulus iuris*. However, according to juridical usage the fact, the purchase, the gift, etc. is designated as the legal title, because we tacitly presuppose the universal legal provision as being self-evident.

5. The question now presents itself: what are the legal titles for acquiring ownership, or as it is also expressed, the rightful title for acquiring ownership?

We distinguish natural and positive legal titles or acquisition titles, according to whether they derive their force from natural or positive law. For example, by the law of the state a person can be provided with an inheritance right which does not have a clear and distinct foundation in the natural law. Likewise, the judge, for example in a distribution case, may establish ownership by *adiudicatio*.

There is another distinction between original and derivative titles for acquisition. The "original" titles to acquisition are the kinds which provide the ownership of a thing to which there was no ownership right up until now. "Derivative" or "derived" ones are those titles to acquisition by virtue of which an already existing ownership right of a person is transferred to another.

We are dealing here with the *natural,* and, in fact in the first instance, with the *original* title to acquisition.

6. There are three *original* titles to acquisition:

Occupatio — taking possession.[6] The reason why this must rate as an acquisitive title is easy to recognize. Every person has the right and the obligation to preserve his life. For that he needs material goods. Thus, he also has a right to use these things. But now the use of a thing presupposes its possession. Furthermore, the possession of a thing which does not yet belong to anyone is represented as taking possession. Thus, each person has the legal authority to take possession of and to occupy material things which are not owned by anyone, i.e. goods without any master.

If taking possession of unowned goods were denied to the person, the right to acquire ownership would thereby be rendered meaningless for him. First ownership could, in any case, not be acquired in any other way than by occupation.

In order that primary occupation may acquire ownership for the person who resorts to it, some conditions must nevertheless be fulfilled.

On the side of the *object,* it is assumed that it is not owned by anyone. For occupation gives rise to ownership but does not destroy it. If the things have already been acquired by someone, the legitimate owner has the right to regard the things as his own, and to exclude everyone else from them. There can be no talk, therefore, of subsequent occupation of a thing that is already owned. Finally, the things themselves are often so designed by nature that it is impossible for them to serve the needs of several persons.[7]

On the part of the person who takes possession, two factors must be in order: the will to acquire the thing as one's own (*animus rem sibi habendi*). For, the intention to own a thing is not identical with the will to possess the thing as property. For example, the owner of a deposit also possesses the object, but he does not wish to possess it as an owner. What is required then is the external sign of an accomplished acquisition of ownership. Since the right of one person always and essentially corresponds to the obligation of another, so, in establishing the first ownership of a thing, the completed acquisition of ownership must be made recognizable by clear signs. An obligation which cannot be known, is, in fact, no obligation. However, what rates as a sign, for example, in hunting, and in fishing, is the actual taking possession of the object; and where land is concerned it is its cultivation, plowing, fencing, etc.[8]

Someone might object: If the ownership of concrete objects is based on occupation and had to be established originally in that way, then the introduction of the entire institution of private property depends on occupation. But now occupation is a free act by a person. Therefore the institution, private property, cannot be designated as a natural one, because what is natural never depends on the free action of a person.

This objection is countered by another equally valid one by Taparelli:[9]

First, I am told: is the fact of a marriage a free act of the person? Certainly. Well then are the marital and parental rights not natural institutions?

Everyone will readily perceive in this example the resolution of the objection. Occupation is a free act for the individual person and in the particular case; but just as in the case of the marital agreement, I regard humanity by and large so that many, indeed, most will perform this free act under the influence and motivation of their rational nature. There may be some who, for higher motivations, will abstain from marriage. But all of humanity will never do this. Now who will designate marriage, because there is not present a necessity which compels all individuals, as an arbitrary arrangement of the human race?[10]

7. The second original title to acquire ownership is *accessio,* accretion. Accretion can take place in two ways: first by nature according to its powers. The natural products of a thing which belong to me become my property. That kind of improvement or increase is, just like the opposite possibility of deterioration, a consequence of the natural qualities of things. He who has acquired this as his

property wanted to have it as it is, and to derive whatever utility from it which it yields of its own nature.[11] Therefore, a growth in value, a "surplus value," can happen to the object which I own, because of social conditions. Thus, for example, the increasing demand for my goods, the expansion of the city, can bring about an increase in the value of may parcel of land, etc.[12] He who was the owner of a thing before the surplus value appeared, still remains the owner after that appeared. Therefore, the newly emerged value accrues to the ownership of the person who until now owned the thing with which that value is associated.

8. The third original title to acquiring property is work: *industria* or *labor*.[13] Man is not the owner of his own personality, because he cannot be his own destiny and his own lord. However, he can use his abilities as his own, so that he has full ownership of the actions stemming from his abilities, and also of their fruits. Now in order that ownership of the fruits of labor is at all practical, it is necessary that the institution, private property, as we concluded earlier,[14] exists in society as a right. At this point we are no longer dealing with the institution of private property in general but with the acquisition of actual ownership of a particular thing. The next question is whether and under what assumptions work can become a title to acquisition. We affirm as follows:

First: work is a real title to acquisition. For a person has the incontestable right to the fruits of his work. These therefore become his property.

Second: work is an *original* title to acquiring ownership. For the fruit of work is something new which arises out of the work, and was therefore not owned by someone else from whom the worker has to derive his ownership right.

Third: But work cannot be the *original* title to acquisition. If a person could create a thing by his work,[15] then the fruit of such activity would have to accrue unconditionally to the ownership of the worker. But man cannot create anything. His activity always presupposes some already existing material as its object, the land which he cultivates, the material to which he gives new form and structure. With this existing material, what is produced by human work is, as a rule, limited very narrowly. Now if the man is to gain as his property the alteration of the material, the new form, the new qualities and capacities which by themselves represent what is created by work, the actual product, the direct fruit of his work, he must at the same time also be the owner of the material itself which became the container of the new form and the new qualities.

Now if the producer himself was already the owner of the land or the material before production took place, then it goes without saying that the product — what has been produced — is also the property of the producer.

If, on the other hand, we are dealing with unowned materials which were made into an object of productive activity, then the processor also acquired ownership of the material, and he does so, in fact, because the work in this instance presupposes occupation; in fact, it may even be regarded as a qualified kind of occupation. — Cathrein[16] shows in a convincing manner why work is not the most original title to acquisition here:

> Let us assume that someone found a piece of wood or a block of marble, and that he carries it home in order to eventually make it into a table or a statue. Can every person come along now and take the piece of wood from him before he begins work on it? Certainly not, any more so than we could take away fish or game from someone who brought it under his control, perhaps even without effort. We do not respond by saying that catching or carrying home is also work. For, if the work, as opposed to merely taking possession, is designated as the original title to acquisition, we understand by this that the work is used for the reshaping and improvement of things. Without any human application, an original acquisition of ownership is in any case impossible. Taking possession of a thing is also a kind of activity. But even in cases where this involves much exertion, as, for example, the long search for and pursuit of wild game, the real title to acquisition is not this prior exertion, but the act of actually taking possession, e.g., the lucky shot or toss. Without this action, no ownership will be acquired despite all effort.

Finally if someone has chosen material which is already owned by someone else as the object of his work, the new form, the reshaping and improving which the product of labor represents, of and by itself belongs to the person who owns the material. The basis for this is clear. The new form, the new qualities, the improvements, constitute a portion of the material and they follow as a part of the ownership of the whole. The fruits which arise in consequence of the working of the soil are furthermore in part a natural increment (*accessio*), to the extent that natural forces and qualities of the field have, in fact, worked along directly in bringing them about. However, the reshaping which material, e.g., the marble, the wood, underwent is, in fact, a merely artificial growth, and it alone traces itself to the work as the principal effect of the change. At the same time the work does not bring about here the ownership of the material, because, viewed in terms of the natural law, it is not a legitimate title to destroy the property, but only to acquire the property, and obviously only where this acquisition is physically and legally possible.

Here we will have to distinguish a threefold assumption:

Someone has worked on an object or processed it consciously without the knowledge and will of the owner, with the understanding that this object is the property of a stranger. That is a case of *mala fides*. No one will acknowledge such work as the legitimate title to acquiring ownership, and he would have to be of the opinion that the injustice itself, the violation of someone else's right, would be capable of establishing a right, i.e., a moral authority, for the person who violated the right.

Let us take another case. Someone in the service of another has planted his field, and processed his raw materials. — Relationships which were not established directly by nature itself can and may in many cases be introduced by the free consent of people. Thus, for example, nothing prevents someone from placing his abilities and strengths in the service of another. On the contrary, this kind of empowerment even constitutes a component of the law by virtue of which a man may dispose of his capacities as something belonging to him. Even the humblest servant has and observes God as the ultimate and highest goal of his life and endeavor, and along with that the inalienable legal claim to all that is a part of true human dignity. However, it by no means contradicts human dignity if one serves another. It is even often true that man in that kind of dependent situation finds a better and more secure preservation of his existence and of the means necessary for it, than if he were left entirely on his own. Now, everywhere that such a positive servant relationship has taken the place of original independence, work ceases to be a title to acquiring direct ownership of physical products of work, because — aside from all else — the product is already produced for the master by force of the legal servant relationship.[17] However, the "fruit of the work," the "yield from labor" for him who uses his strength in the service of another, is the just wage which must be provided on the basis of those services by workers.

The third assumption would be: someone has processed this material of someone else, or reprocessed it *bona fide*, i.e., without knowing that the material which he made the object of his work belonged to someone else. — In this case it is fitting, even if not according to the requirements of strict justice, nevertheless out of honesty, that under certain assumptions the ownership of the material of the other person accrues to the producer, whereby he must recompense the previous owner. Therefore, positive law has often ruled in this way. Thus, for example, Roman law[18] in its principles about "specification," i.e., changing the form of a thing by work. He who has processed material belonging to another in such a way that it emerges as a new thing, has acquired ownership of this new thing, and with it also of the material. The restructuring must be a thorough-going kind, so that the former structure cannot be reproduced, and the thing emerges as something different as viewed by business. Mere destruction or coloring, e.g., would not be sufficient, and also not the threshing of grain. If one's own material is used at the same time as that of someone else, then according to Roman law the worker acquires ownership of the whole, new thing even in the case that perhaps the old form could be reproduced. — Germanic law of the Middle Ages went further than Roman law, since it established the principle that to derive the fruits, he who "earned" them is justified in owning them, i.e., he who accomplished the work necessary for deriving it.[19] That principle came to apply for: 1) the person who at the time the work was done had the right to enjoy the fruit, but whose right ended before the fruit was available; 2) he who in good faith planted the field of another by mistake. With the adoption of Roman law, this principle was generally done away with. It was retained in lien law[20] and in some particular laws, e.g., in Saxony and partially in Prussian land laws.

9. Previously we distinguished between original and derivative titles to acquiring ownership. We have yet to deal with the latter.

There are two kinds of derivative acquisition and acquisitive titles: hereditary and contractual.

For hereditary succession we distinguish between intestate succession and testamentary succession.

The justification for ownership lies in its purpose. However, property ownership is supposed to serve also and especially the purposes of the family — as we indicated earlier. The purposes of the family do not die with the head of the family or the individual family member. They continue so long as the family itself lasts. Charles Périn says:[21]

Since the family is not destined to last for just one generation, and since it is supposed to carry on in succeeding generations all of the social virtues and traditions of which it is the bearer, therefore property ownership must continue and be able to be transmitted from the father to those who bear his name and continue his personage. By the inheritance right the moral entity which the family constitutes must preserve itself and be able to extend itself further according to its merits. It is from this that the inheritance right stemmed, and it retained the same sanction as the right of property ownership in all societies where the natural law of human life is observed.

Thus, the members of the family, aside from all wills, have a right by natural law to inheritance, even if this right calls for more direct expression in various ways by positive legislation.[22]

Just like the intestate succession of family members, so too testamentary succession likewise finds its foundation in the natural law. The head of the family has paternal authority by virtue of which he can determine, with regard to the family members, in what manner the wealth can be made to serve the domestic common interests. This paternal authority, however, is like the jurisdictional authority of the ruler in the state. As the will of the lawmaker in state laws also continues after his death since the law has as its basis and purpose not the individual welfare of the ruler, but the general interests of the nation, that is also the case with the father of the family as such. He is to take the kind of action in the interest of the family welfare with regard to wealth that is intimately associated with the family, as should first take effect for the time after his death.[23] However, it is not only the head of the family as such who has the right of testamentary disposal. Also other persons may determine by testamentary rules to whom the ownership of their wealth or parts of it are to be transmitted. We may establish the legal validity of these last will proclamations in various ways: first, by the *consensus* between the testator and the heirs. The will of the testator lasts morally after his death; the will of the heirs enter in also. A physical coexistence of the two will proclamations is not called for by any contract. As the master of a thing can give it away or throw it away, so he may also during his lifetime reach a determination that one of the persons designated by him may take precedence over all others in the appropriation of what is left. Thus, the legal validity of the last will arrangements — aside from all concerns of honesty, piety, etc. — appears to be required in a certain way by the public welfare. For example, if there were not the right of the testator to make a will, then all of the goods which he owned at the moment of his death would become the property of the negative community of goods, i.e., it would be without an owner. But that would contradict the social need and purpose for which ownership the distribution of goods had to be introduced: social peace, order, and the proper care of material goods.

But could not all of such goods be turned over to the state? No matter how we may wish to appraise the advantages of state ownership within certain limits, we nevertheless hold that an excessive expansion of that could not be reconciled with the general welfare of the people. Reasons similar to the ones which we adduced against socialistic or communistic forms of society support our view on this. Therefore, in cases where the testator failed to arrange for the disposition of his wealth, and where there are no natural heirs, the state may assume ownership of the inheritance for itself. Furthermore, in the interest of the common good, the state may apply the greatest care in devising a legislative structure of inheritance that conforms with the natural law. However, we may not, like Bluntschli among others, seek to extend the "subsidiary inheritance right" of the state in a manner which allows us to forget that the state is here for people, and that the political order has its purpose in the civil order.

It may be argued: since the goods do not transmit to the ownership of the heirs without his will, so they may still be ownerless goods until the *acceptatio* by the heirs, from the moment of the death of the testator.[24] — We respond: first, it is an error to assume that a person cannot acquire any right without his consent.

Every person has from nature, for example, the right to make use of his life and his strength; every person has the right to his good name and his honor, without having to formally acknowledge that. Thus, in our case we are not dealing with a *ius in re,* but solely with a *ius ad rem.* The person will acquire no right to ownership without his consent; but nothing stands in the way of his right to acquire ownership specifically of some particular goods without his consent, just as every person has received this right already from nature, without his having to express his willingness.

10. The second derivative title to acquisition is the contract. From the nature of the property right there arises for the owner the authority to dispose of the things which belong to him, in every moral permissible manner. Therefore he may also assign to another, by a contract, what was until then his property and actually transfer it to him.

The contract is an agreement of the wills of two or more persons in a binding manner to establish or change legal circumstances. For the concluding of a contract, an agreement of the wills of the contracting parties is required with regard to the essential parts of the contract, and also with a statement of the binding intention and the declaration of the consensus of both parties. A contract would be invalid where it is drawn up without the necessary freedom of one of the parties. Not every kind of extrinsic or intrinsic necessity negates the contract, but only the kind where the requisite deliberation is absent or the extrinsic declaration does not allow the expression of the will to appear. Therefore the contract concluded under the influence of severe and unjust duress is null (*irritus*), or at least it may be dissolved (*rescindibilis*). — Also invalid is a contract which by its content requires what is physically or morally impossible. Moral impossibility is present, however, if the contracting party lacks the authority to act in a particular manner, or if the contracting party, as such, does have the right to make such a disposition, but not under the prevailing circumstances. — Thus, a contract is invalid where it is concluded by the contracting parties, or by one of them, under the dominion of an essential error with regard to the substance or the peculiar properties of the contracted object.

For turning over property the following come under consideration: gifts, loans, purchases and sales. In economic life the loan and the purchase in particular are of the greatest importance. —

All contracts which deal with an exchange in the broadest sense, i.e., where a service and a reciprocal service are involved, are under the dominion of the *principle of equivalence* : performance and reciprocal performance must be *equal in value.* Taparelli established clearly and concisely the principle of equivalence in the following manner:

> Wherein does the will of the contracting party consist in bilateral contracts? They do not intend a gift, but only an exchange, i.e., to acquire an equivalent for the thing given up. Now if the freedom of the one party is surrendered or diminished either by deception or by force or intimidation, etc., and if more is taken from him than he intended to give up, then this violation of equivalency is just as much an unjust acquisition as the purse stolen by the robber, which the traveler gave him to save his life. It is something else if this exceeding of equivalence is freely allowed by the contracting parties; for since each is the master of his transferable rights, so the natural law cannot prevent the transfer of such rights.[25]

11. Among contracts which transfer ownership, the *loan contract* calls for more detailed treatment.

The loan is a transfer of a thing according to weight, number, or size to another, of the sort where the thing is turned over to the ownership of the other, along with the obligation of later returning a thing of the same kind and of the same worth.

a) It is the conferral of a thing (*traditio rei*). The loan, in fact, appears as a real contract by which a promise to lend may perhaps be prearranged, but which is first concluded by turning over the object. The external basis for it is the manner of looking at it, as that always applied in commerce and law. Thus, the loan is the first of the four known real contracts in Roman law. An intrinsic basis is derived from the purpose of the loan. Of itself the loaned object is given for the purpose of use, but the possibility of the use presupposes the ownership of the thing. Finally, from the essential obligation of the loan there can be no talk of a repayment before the transfer and the receipt of the object loaned.

b) The loan is surrender of a thing that is estimated according to weight, number, or size. Things which tend to be evaluated in commerce on an individual basis, e.g., a field, a house, etc., do not constitute the objects of the loan contract; but what is involved here solely are the kinds of objects which can be represented because of their generic or specific similarities as of the same species and kind for the purposes of exchange (*res fungibiles*). From the interchangeability, therefore, we arrive of necessity at the conclusion that in the exchange of such things it is their quantity (size,number, weight) in the first instance, and only secondarily the quality which is taken into consideration. Practice has come to understand the fungibility of loan objects in such a way that only such things are the objects of an actual loan contract which are consumed at the first use of them (*res primo usu consumptibiles*), whether their use implies a natural consumption associated with the physical destruction of the thing, e.g., the use of food articles, or only a *civilis consumptio* by their distribution, e.g., a sum of money. It is a simple conclusion from what has been said, that if the object of the loan became the object of the contract as an infertile thing, what is consumed by its first use, what ceases to exist physically or morally, cannot of itself directly serve the purposes of yielding earnings.

c. The loan immediately transfers the ownership of the loaned object to the debtor, and it is a true disposition of the thing. This happens first of all from the purpose of the contract. A fungible thing and one that is consumed by its first use is hereby transferred in such a way that the actual use and consumption is turned over to the debtor Now how is the creditor supposed to retain and be able to assert ownership of such a thing? Note well: it is only essential that the debtor has the right to use; whether he actually makes use of this right is of no consequence for the contract, any more than are the different kinds of consumption. Whether he wishes to drink the wine I loaned him, or sell it, is his business. The purpose of the surrender of the object is principally the distinguishing mark between the loan and the other real contracts which were mentioned. The purpose of the deposit (*depositum*) is the safety of the thing, and the purpose of the loan (*commodatum*) is its use (without consumption); and the pledge (*pignus*) finally is the safeguarding of the right to demand. The variety in the purposes is determined by the variety of the legal consequences of the surrender, which for the loan extends ownership, and for the other real contracts provides only possession.

The ownership transfer of the loaned object is the real basis why people of the Middle Ages did not want to acknowledge that by the transfer of money to another in the loan transaction, one got to share in the profit which such other person could make with the money. No one who sells an egg can any longer rightfully make a claim to the cake. If the sum that was loaned out went over to the ownership of the debtor, then obviously the creditor no longer had a claim to the fruits to which the property of another and the work of another gave rise. The juridically incontestable doctrine of the transfer of ownership of the loaned sum to the debtor in fact proclaims and establishes the canonical ban on interest taking. The earliest opponents of the canonical ban on interest understood this very well. — The humanist Joachim Camerarius,[26] for example, in order to justify interest on capital denied precisely the transfer of the ownership of the loaned sum to the debtor. Only the use, making use of it, was transferred to the debtor, and for this use a price could therefore be charged, as for the use of a house or of an animal. We could raise the objection against the transfer of ownership: the creditor adds the debt amount to his assets, and the debtor, to his liabilities; therefore no actual transfer of value seems to have taken place. Without a transfer of value, however, there is no transfer of ownership. The refutation of this objection is not difficult. For, the fact that we have ascribed to our own wealth a sum that is owed to us, by no means signifies that we necessarily retain a right to the same individual pieces and their actual value. No creditor has a right to the thing (*ius in re*) with regard to a particular piece of the wealth of the debtor, but only a right to the thing (*ius ad rem similem eiusdem speciei et qualitatis*), a personal claim against the debtor. Also, in the various forms of mobilizing the claims which the credit economy of our time has come up with: checks, stocks, bonds, deposit certificates, bank notes, etc., the value of the claim associated with the paper is in a certain way essentially relative, nothing more than a prospective thing — the prospect of getting the actual value of some future performance. Everything else lies within the realm of the juridical and economic imagination; commercial paper is an object of value only by virtue of the functions which commerce has assigned to it. Incidentally, the part which now follows the definition of the loan contract established above will be able to affirm further what has been said.

d) The debtor takes over the obligation to repay a thing of the same kind or of the same worth.

He first of all assumes the obligation to restore a thing of equal value; otherwise we would not be dealing with a loan, but at least in part, with a gift.

The object of the restoration is a thing of the same kind and worth. It thereby allows the return of another individual thing which is first of all numerically a different thing than what was received. For if the purpose of the transfer is the use of the thing, naturally this thing which no longer exists after its use can no longer be returned. This other thing must nevertheless be of the same kind and species. The creditor receives a thing in return which is not only a fungible, usable thing, but also fungible and usable with the consequence of the transfer of ownership and of the debtor's right to use it. The creditor awaits a return by virtue of the agreement, and in fact, a return of a thing of the same kind; if he were to require money in place of the grain which he loaned, then we are no longer talking about a loan but about a purchase; and if he demanded in place of the one commodity another commodity, grain for oil, then we have an exchange, not a loan agreement. The object to be returned must be of the same kind, but also of the same value. In every contract where a thing is given for another thing, and where the party does not have the intention of making a gift, — briefly in every contract which comes down to an exchange in any way — justice requires a corresponding equality between what is given and what is gotten. This equality (*aequalitas permutationis*) is, as already indicated, the highest law of fair exchange. Where we are dealing with fungible things It involves mainly quantity: it involves an equality of size, number, or weight. Nevertheless, differing specific qualities and degrees of perfection can be present in the various individual pieces of the same kind, and this means then that there is at the same time a difference in the intrinsic value of the objects in question. The value appraisal of fungible things is therefore also determined according to quality; and just as the repayment of an equal quantity (of a *tantundem*), the return of the equal quality (of a *tantundem eiusdem qualitatis*) is a demand of commutative justice, because that is necessary to preserve the *aequalitas permutationis.* Only the equal value between what is given and what is gotten in return satisfies the *principle of equivalence* in exchange transactions,which was always defended by the Scholastics and by Canon Law.

Here, however, we must refer to the distinction between money and other goods in loan transactions. For objects which were not money, the natural worth, the intrinsic value, was taken into account. For example whoever gave a measure of grain to another as a loan, gets in return a measure of equally good grain, even if in the meantime the market price of such grain had changed: risen or fallen. With money, however, only the extrinsic value or value of the coin on the market is taken into account. Even though the intrinsic value of the coin, insofar as it is minted of precious metal of one or the other degree of fineness, is the basis for determining its extrinsic value, then in ordinary commerce what is taken into account, first of all, is not so much this material value as the formal value which the coin has as a universal measure of value and of price, in other words, as money. He who gave a loan of 100 marks, receives the value of 100 marks in return in such a way, in fact, that the coin used to repay, whatever kind it may be, is calculated according to its value on the exchange. There remains one last factor in the definition of the loan contract.

e) The debtor is obligated only to provide repayment later on. This too emanates of necessity from the purpose of the loan. That involves providing the debtor with something that he can use or consume. Therefore he must be given time to do so. The immediate repayment of the same, or of an equivalent thing would make the whole loan contract illusory. Therefore the loan is called a bilateral agreement (*contractus bilateralis*) — an agreement with reciprocal obligation. The creditor is obligated to not demand the repayment before the time that is established or that is to be established; the debtor, in return must complete repayment at the right time.

It is not hard to explain the canonical ban on interest in terms of this approach.

By *usura* or unjust interest was understood any gain which the creditor derives from the loan and, in fact, demands because of the loan owed by the borrower.[27]

It was a profit, i.e., something that could be appraised in money, whether it is money itself, or a service, an obligation, etc.

A profit from the loan; thus not from any other agreement, e.g., a business agreement, a rental agreement, etc.

A profit by virtue of the loan; that is to say not by virtue of a title extrinsic to the loan, e.g., the restoration of loss, or for a certain risk, etc.

A profit which was required as a debt by virtue of the loan. Accordingly, if the loan was only the pretext and the motivation for the debtor to voluntarily give something to the creditor, not to meet his strict obligation, but to fulfill an obligation in gratitude, then, likewise, according to the broadest understanding, there was no *usura* — no usury in the objectionable sense.

However, interest demanded by virtue of the loan itself rated as usury. Why? The demand and the debt appeared according to the principle of equivalence for just exchange transactions in the form of an equation. The equal sign which signified equal value here may never become a lie. Where it surrenders its truth, usury begins. The creditor should get back what he gave or offered; and the debtor should not have to pay more than he received, or what the creditor offered him. The lender gave 100. If he asks for 110 back, then he is asking for more than he is entitled to. He enriches himself at the expense of someone else's property, and that was usury, an obvious violation of the *aequalitas permutationis*. The reasoning of St. Thomas Aquinas[28] also applies in this matter: it is against justice to sell the same thing twice, or to sell something that is nothing in itself. But the interest collector does something of both. Either he receives the usurious interest for the object loaned itself, or for its use. In the first case he sells the same thing twice, or he receives a doubled price for the object loaned, the repayment of the capital, along with the interest. In the second case, he get a price for something whose value, taken by itself, cannot be estimated. The use of a thing which is destroyed by its use is lost, is consumed, has no value different from the thing itself. This was always and indeed juridically correct, it was assumed that fungible things and in fact, consumable ones, were the objects of the loan and furthermore that a real transfer of ownership of those things was accomplished by the contract.

The loan in itself can therefore of its nature not be a lucrative business. This juridical and philosophically incontestable principle, however, by no means prevented the right to demand, on the basis of special titles in individual cases, an additional amount, all the less so as, above all, the legal claim to recompense for sacrifices that were really made and measurable in money is likewise a requirement of commutative justice, just as is the equivalence in the value between what is given and what is gotten in an exchange transaction. Therefore it would be an indication of what is only superficial knowledge of the canonical ban on interest if we want to look at the introduction of titles to interest as an abandonment of the earlier point of view, and as a concession made to the emerging capitalism, instead of as the logical, consistent following through and adaptation of the great law of business — commutative justice — to the growing commerce.

We have to limit ourselves here to the most urgent indications, even though a deeper study of the "titles to interest" may be very instructive.

St. Thomas already developed the basic justification of the so-called *risk premium. Res, quae extra periculum possidentur eiusdem speciei, plus aestimantur, quam eaedem in periculo existentes.*[29] The danger diminishes the value of the endangered thing. Accordingly the risk premium assumes the character of a compensation, of a *usura compensatoria,* which was recognized throughout by the Scholastics, as much as the *usura lucratoria* for the loan was universally condemned by them. But what kind of danger must there be so that the sum loaned out would lose in value by it, and thereby establish a quasi-restitution claim?[30] The danger must first of all be *genuine* and *extraordinary.* Above all, what is not enough is that most general danger which applies to all goods, of being destroyed by elemental forces, or by people out of malice, or pilfered, so long as the transfer of money to the debtor does not increase this and similar general dangers in any special way. Furthermore, it is also not the danger that is involved in every loan as such.

> If a sum of money is turned over to someone else for safekeeping in a sealed purse, the owner trusts in the honesty of the other; but assuming this, the fate of the fortune of the recipient is immaterial to him. For even if that latter is impoverished, the sealed purse is still always found with him, and it is restored to the owner by replevin. Not so if the same sum of money is given out on loan; for now if the honest recipient becomes insolvent, the money is lost to the donor. Thus, the greater danger which the giver subjects himself to by the loan, independent of the honest intention of the recipient, is based on the fact that the giver turned over ownership of the money, so that he has surrendered the protection involved in the replevin.[31]

However, also these particular dangers peculiar to the loan, as opposed to other kinds of contracts like the deposit, the *commodatum,* etc. remain within the limits of *periculum commune et ordinarium* are dangers which are instrinsically inseparable from a loan which by no means suffice to justify any extra compensation because of *periculum sortis.* Alfonsus of Ligouri even requires for this that the danger is not only the *verum* and *extraordinarium* kind, but that it must be even a *periculum probabtiliter imminens.*[32] Then and only then can there be talk of money that is loaned and which loses in value, so that the creditor thereby makes a sacrifice which is measurable at the very moment the loan is made. It is in the nature of the thing that this title to interest had to come into the picture in trade during earlier times. —

Another title to interest — indeed the one that is most important practically, is the claim to replacement of *interest*, of *id quod interest*.[33] When the creditor suffered a loss or lost some profit by the loan, he could demand recompense. At least the *titulus damni emergentis*, the claim to recompense for loss, is certain, said St. Alphonsus. But there was not always the same certainty with regard to the *titulus lucri cessantis*. The *damnum emergens* is actually the loss of existing real value which is in itself definite and measurable; the *lucrum cessans*, as the object of a loss of earning prospects, generally represents a future value, a value which is still conditional in some respects with regard to its actual existence, and which therefore appears uncertain, as anything in the future is uncertain for a person. Yet, the *titulus lucri cessantis* was nevertheless universally recognized; but what were the prerequisites? By the loan itself the creditor must actually have had to be placed in a position where he could not make use of his money for an actually existing, not merely imagined purpose, with regard to some other profit-making investment of his money on the basis of an objectively existing possibility. Only the reference to a concrete and definite transaction which is in prospect, for whose operation the creditor wanted to and could use precisely this money which he now lends to the debtor, justifies the claim to recompense because of lost profit. If the creditor had other money available which he could have used for transacting that particular business, he could not make a claim to recompense; just any loss at all would not allow itself to be traced back so much to the loan relationship, but rather to the decision of the creditor to not make use of such other disposable money. To what extent the *titulus lucri cessantis* presupposes a form that is conceivable in its concrete form, and in what is at least in its consequences a somehow calculable, determinate transaction, is clear from the fact that it required that the profit of such a transaction was not to be computed at its full amount in the interest rate, but *iuxta aestimationem spei et periculi et deductis expensis*, and according to a well-established view, also with the deduction of a wage for one's own eventual labor involved in it. That is the *titulus lucri cessantis* as seen by the old moralists. — Obviously this title had to be applied more and more in commerce, especially at the time when, with the blossoming of manufacturing, money took on a more important role for production, and found more frequent "productive application." Incidentally, the title to interest was by no means discovered by the Scholastics, but instead the Roman legal doctrine of recompense for interest in the loan relationships was applied.

The final title to interest: interest for *delay, conventional penalty,* does not cause any difficulty in principle. In Scholastic teaching, the conventional penalty is not, like the other titles, a means to replace loss, whose legitimacy and limits could be ascertained from the preservation of some *aequalitas permutationis;* but instead it was simply a contractually arranged, moderate penalty for egregious and negligent failure to observe the agreed upon terms on the part of the debtor. The conventional penalty is essentially a punishment, and it is to be viewed as such. Therefore where there is no guilt, whether in the form of deception, or of crass negligence, the conventional penalty may not be invoked. The *poena conventionalis* becomes a case which calls for mandatory restitution for "usury in the terms," as soon as it is required not only as a means to enforce the contract, but with the intention of making a profit. For that would add up to an unjust enrichment for the creditor, without any title. That kind of intention is to be presumed when the creditor deliberately sets the terms in such a way that the debtor could not observe them, so that he would be liable to the penalties through no fault of his own.

12. Now that represents the so often misunderstood, and so carelessly condemned, doctrine of Canon Law about lending and interest, which is nevertheless not refuted by anyone even to this time. In practice the Church does not wish to combat moderate interest-taking today, but also without in some way taking back its teaching on interest on loans. The attempt was made to explain this by saying that the Church in its great moderation sought to avoid a greater evil, since opposition is practically useless. We must unconditionally oppose this explanation from the theological point of view as irreconcilable with the sanctity of the Church. If taking interest is under present-day conditions really still the same frightful crime it was designated as and treated by the Church in times past, then the Church cannot be silent, and much less allow Church institutes to take interest. No, the present-day position of the Church can be explained solely by the fact that under present economic conditions taking interest involves in itself no violation of commutative justice. Those who have money in our time have as a rule at their disposal in fact the real opportunity to make profit. Now on the basis of these conditions we may impute to anyone who gives money out on loan a title to interest, since he deprives himself of the opportunity to make money, for the advantage of another, to a degree that can be measured in monetary terms, and that he may therefore claim recompense in interest. Or we may see in the interest the price for the possibility of making profit provided by the loan.[34] In both explanations it is the principle of equivalence which under present conditions justifies moderate interest-taking. At any rate complete freedom to charge interest,

considered economically, is a powerful evil — the birthplace of modern capitalism. But it is an evil which naturally attaches itself to the evil of the free economy.

We refer here briefly to a view which Ratzinger presented in the second edition of his *Volkswirtschaft* .[35] Ratzinger distinguishes for present-day conditions between loans which may not require interest, and remunerative credit..

> Where money is given for a momentary need and it passes to the ownership of the borrower, it is not allowed to charge interest for the use of the money. The case is different where the money is sought as the equivalent of a means of production, so as to seek surplus value in combination with work. Here we are dealing with a capital transaction, and recompense can be claimed for providing credit. That money transaction (loan) is to be distinguished from the capital transaction (credit).... We can only speak of credit where a higher value is sought for the future with the loaned cash.... In credit, unlike in a loan, the ownership is not transferred to the borrower, but only its temporary use as capital is authorized. The credit-giver carries, with the lack of a pledge, the risk of losing all of the value in the future. This is a decisive point to which St. Thomas Aquinas already drew attention, etc.

We do not share this view. Even in present-day credit- or capital - transactions there is still a loan in terms of its intrinsic meaning. The ownership of the actual sum that is loaned goes over the the credit-taker. The creditor has no property right to any part of the wealth of his debtor. All that remains with him is a personal claim to the eventual return of the same amount. At any rate the assumption of the risk is a decisive point for the judgment of the present-day credit transaction. But precisely this point shows that the "capital transaction" too is no different kind of business than the loan. For, juridically the creditor in no way bears the risk of the enterprise for which the borrowed money is used. If the enterprise fails or if the borrower encounters full economic ruin, the creditor still has a claim against the debtor, and he can make that claim if the debtor again gets some wealth. It is also juridically inadmissible to regard the "interest" from the credit transaction as a share of the profit quota. The creditor has no share in the business, and therefore also no share in the profit. The authority of St. Thomas to which Ratzinger appeals does not speak for, but against, his approach.[36] The Holy Doctor distinguishes between the loan and the business contract. He writes about the qualities involved in taking over the risk of the loan, which are found also in present-day credit transactions, whereas the "capital transaction" of Ratzinger does not correspond to present-day credit transactions. It represents instead a social condition. If the abnormalities of the free economy are one day overcome, and mere possession of cash money does not provide for itself that extraordinary facility for making profit by sharing in capital associations, by production, speculation, etc., only then will the time have come when interest on loans will again be restricted, and where the social contract can in large measure represent that. This is also the point of view which the Congress of Italian Catholics, held in Rome under the tutelage of Cardinal Parocchi, adopted on the subject when it declared: "It is very important to turn into an associate the capitalist who lends money to the industrialist, who then shares the risk of the enterprise in the likeness of a limited partnership, so as to reduce the class of the capitalists who are really nothing more than lenders of money."[37]

13. In conclusion a few words yet about the *praescriptio,* the acquisition by prescription [38] i.e., the acquisition of actual ownership of someone else's thing by means of possession in good faith over a long duration. *Praescriptio* is of a positive-legal nature. Its legislative introduction, however, appears in the interest of continuing peace in social life, and because there is a feeling that it is very effective for commercial security. In cases where *praescriptio* gets applied, it is the law, the public authority which has dominion. But in order that the acquisition of property by prescription may take place, the fulfillment of certain conditions is usually required by legislation. The thing itself must be capable of prescription. A thing which is generally excluded from private ownership can also not be acquired by prescription. On the part of the one who exercises the right, good faith is required. If that is lacking, and if the one who holds the object complains that what is happening is unjust, then also the passage of time will not be enough to make what is wrong, right. Finally, the possession of the thing should be a kind of possession which corresponds to the alleged property right. Therefore it must be based on a clearly correct title to acquisition, so that the occupier could actually own the thing in good faith. Then there must be continuous occupation without interruption for a longer period of time.[39]

¹Cf. our previous discussions, p. 213f.

²At any rate, the original *communio bonorum* has, along with the negative factors (the fact that nature did not make any distribution of goods), also a positive factor inasmuch as the natural law provided all with the capacity to use everything and to acquire it as property, so long as it had not yet been taken possession of by others. Cf. Lessius, *De iustitia et iure lib.* 2, c.5, n.4.

³This is not to deny that occupation took place not only by the individual, *distributive,* but also by many together (a tribe etc.), *collective.* Whether and to what extent this happened in reality — that is a purely historical question.

⁴Cf. above, p 210ff.

⁵*Moralphilosophie* I (3rd ed.), 490f.

⁶The difficulty which we already discussed, to the effect that a fact cannot be a legal basis for property, is resolved by Liberator (*Grundsätze der Volkwirtschaft* [Innsbruck 1891] p. 183), with regard to occupation, in that he distinguishes between the determinative and the legitimizing principle of property in the following manner: "The legitimizing principle of property is *nature* which equipped man for dominion over the lesser things that are given for his use and suited providentially and socially, and as a result, for permanent ownership. By occupation nothing happens but that such possession with regard to things which belong to no one else, and which we may therefore take without infringing on anyone else, was firmly established. And it is a peculiarity of that right which arises from nature in an imprecise and abstract manner, so that it can become concrete and individualized only by a fact. The agreement of marriage partners is a fact; and and it nevertheless establishes marital rights in a concrete manner. Procreation is a fact; and at the same time it establishes paternal rights in particular. The same happens here: occupation is a fact, but it is of a kind which serves to establish a right that is given to a man in an indeterminate manner." — For the sake of greater clarity we distinguish a twofold "legitimizing principle": 1. the legal basis for the institution, private property, which is given with the adduced reasons for the necessity and justification of property; 2. the legal provision, which explains certain kinds of facts in general as being suited by natural law for acquiring concrete ownership. And with that, we occupy ourselves at this point, where proof is presented that occupation, work, etc. are those kinds of facts, and they can therefore change the indeterminate right to acquire property into a materially determinate right.

⁷Even today there are still objects which have no owner, and where the rightful title of first occupation can apply, e.g., the wildlife in the field and forest, the birds in the air, the fish in the great rivers and oceans, fruits which grow wild, etc. — Likewise jurisprudence includes herein the *res derelictae,* things which have been given up by their owners with the idea that they no longer want them. (The mere surrender of possession without that intention is not yet a surrender of ownership. We have in mind, for example, the goods which were tossed overboard of a ship in order to lighten the load.) Also included here is the treasure which has been hidden for so long, that no one can claim it any more as property.

[8]Cf. A. M. Weiss, O. Pr. *Sociale Frage und sociale Ordnung* I (3rd ed.) 371. "Even the so-called *first occupation* is not a mere declaration of intention but an actual application of bodily and intellectual energies. The notion of the socialists that ownership settled from an effortless declaration of intention, at most from a court document, is childish to a great degree, and it smacks more of cafe humor than of what we should expect from them. We would think that it should be clear to them most of all that the first cultivation of the soil or the sinking of a mine shaft could not happen without intense physical and mental exertion, and that this work is merely the forerunner of thousands of others."

[9]*Op. cit.* Nr. 409. — Cf. also Cathrein, *Moralphilosophie* II (3rd ed.) 292.

[10]Cf. above, p. 295 with fn. 2. Note how our proofs for the institution, private property, distinguish carefully between natural justification, to acquire stable ownership as this applies to the individual person, and, on the other hand, the natural necessity of private property which is affirmed and demonstrated for all of society.

[11]Taparelli, *op. cit.* I, nr. 412. — It is also in conformity with reason that, what is a part of the things which belong to me, even if it is not the product of what I own, is nevertheless my property, insofar as it may be regarded as something that is related as an accessory, to things which belong to me. "*Accessorium sequitur principale.* " For complex cases, positive law must determine what is to rate as the main thing, and how, in general, the more proximate determinations of acquisition of private property is a matter for positive law, like *alluvio, commixtio, etc.*

[12]Cf. *Kölner Korrespondenz,* published by Dr. P. Oberdörffer, 7th yr. vol. 2/3, p. 38.

[13]But it is not the *sole* title to acquisition. The socialists teach, following the lead of liberal philosophers and economists: each person has a claim only to the product of his labor.

[14]Cf. p. 270ff.

[15]Creation is "*productio rei ex nihilo sui et ex nihilo* subiecti, *et ex nihilo* sui," i.e., it has to be something which did not exist before; "*ex nihilo* subiecti:" this *something* cannot be merely a new form or the restructuring of matter which was already on hand.

[16]*Moralphilosophie* II (3rd ed.) 303.

[17]We do not say that Leo XIII, with the statement: "As effects follow their cause, so it is just and right that the results of labor should belong to him who has labored" (*R. N.* 8), somehow wants to acknowledge in a certain socialistic sense the ownership of the products of labor also for the worker who works in the service of others. The assumption would be too naive. The Pope then acknowledged in the same breath the exclusive and permanent property right of the same to the first one to acquire a thing — a right of which the Pope says that no one may violate "it in any way;" even while, at the same time again affirming the assignment of the object by the application of labor, and as the fruit of the same, to the rightful owner. — Furthermore, the encyclical recognizes once again the wage relationship as such, as conforming to justice. — The fact is that by the above statement, the Pope simply wants to establish the right of property in principle and abstractly. He is thereby abstracting from the accessory conditions which arise with a contract, and from the legal consequences of those. Where he speaks about the wage relationship, the "fruit of labor" in the juridical sense is also the wage according to Leo XIII.

[18]Cf. I, 7, §7; I. 9, §1; I. 26, 3. *Dig. de acquirendo rerum dominio* 41, 1. — L. 13; I. 14, *Dig. de cond. furtiva* 13, I; I. 12, *Dig. ad exhibend.* 10, 4.

[19]Cf., as opposed to this, I. 25, 1, *Dig. de usuris* 22, 1.

[20]II *Feud.* ^3.

[21]*Christliche Politik.* 1st half (Freiburg 1876) p. 202.

[22]The teaching of St. Thomas Aquinas on this matter, cf. in Franz Schaub, *Eigenthumslehre* (Freiburg 1898) p. 302f. 374ff. — Bluntschli (*Staatswörterbuch* [1858]) p. 321 states: "The right of inheritance preserves ownership and ennobles it. The accomplishments of the ancestors is transferred to the successors by the inheritance right, and the industry of the father is increased by the prospect that he can still extend benefits to his children. The cohesion of the family derives its support and its economic expression through the inheritance right." — By "members of the family" are meant first of all the children of the testator. But also the more distant members constitute a component of the family. Therefore, the more the idea of the unity of the family gains recognition, the more reasonable it is in the event that there are no children, to include other relatives in the inheritance. For, even the deceased member of the family got from the family his existence, his strength. Therefore it is proper that what he acquired by this strength, reverts to the family, first to the parents, if these are still living, and then to their heirs, the brothers and sisters of the deceased, etc.

[23]Cf. Card. de Lugo, *De iustitia et iure* D. 3, n. 17: "*Sicut dominium iurisdictionis datur cum ea amplitudine, ut possit princeps nunc lege sua obligare pro tempore futuro eos, qui nunc non sunt eius subditi, immo nec nati; quia nimirum ad perfectam rei publicae administrationem, quam hic homo nunc habet, pertinet, providere etiam pro tempore futuro, et ideo summus Pontifex disponit de modo eligendi successores suos pro tempore futuro, quia hoc spectat etiam ad ecclesiae gubernationem: sic dominium proprietatis dat facultatem disponendi de re, quae nunc est sub tuo dominio pleno, etiam pro tempore future, quo non iam sis eius dominus.*"

[24]Cf. Schiffini I. c. p. 197.

[25]*Versuch eines auf Erfahrung begründeten Naturrechts* I (Regensburg 1845), 486f. with the footnote. Taparelli adds, — the positive law can at times add precautionary rules to the natural law, and those kinds of safeguards are very apropos in our case (to safeguard justice in contractual activities).

[26]*Politics* 61ff.

[27]Cf. on this matter: Benedict XIV, Encyclical *Vix Perventi* to the bishops of Italy, 1 November 1745: "*Peccati genus illud, quod usura vocatur, quodque in contractu mutui propriam suam sedem et locum habet, in eo est repositum, quod quis ex ipsomet mutuo (quod suapte natura tantundem dumtaxat reddi postulat, quantum receptum est) plus sibi reddi velit, quam est receptum ideoque ultra sortem lucrum aliquod, ipsius ratione mutui, sibi deberi contendat.*" On the "ecclesiastical concept of usury," etc. cf. the *Referat des k. k. Finanzrathes Dr. Karl Scheimpflug f. d. Leo-Gesellschaft in Wien, Section für Socialwissenschaften*, 1892.

[28]*S. Th.* 2,2, q.78, a.1.

[29]*S. Th. opusc.* 75, c.6.

[30]S. Alphons. I. 3, tr. 5, n. 764.

[31]v. Savigny, *System des römischen Rechts* V, 514.

[32]*Lib.* 3, tr. 5, n. 764 (8).

[33]S. Alphons. I. c. 768ff.

[34]The price theory developed by us in the Innsbruck "*Zeitschift für katholische Theologie* " XII, 36ff. 393aff. was also presented in detail by Palmieri in *Antonii Ballerini, Opus theol. morale* III (Prati 1890) 652ff.

[35]Cf. Dr. G. Ratzinger, *Die Volkswirtschaft in ihren sittlichen Grundlagen* (2nd fully revised edition, Freiburg 1895) p. 10. 264ff.

[36]The passage in Thomas (*S. theol.*   2,2,q.78, a.2 *ad* 5) reads: "*Ille, qui mutuat pecuniam, transfert dominium pecuniae in eum, cui mutuat; unde ille, cui pecunia mutuatur, sub suo periculo tenet eam et tenetur eam restituere integre. Unde non debet amplius exigere ille, qui mutuavit. — Se ille, qui committit pecuniam suam vel mercatori vel artifici per modum societatis cuiusdam, non transfert dominium pecuniae suae in illum, sed remanet eius; ita quod cum periculo ipsius mercator de eo negotiatur vel artifex operatur; et ideo sic licite potest partem lucri inde provenientis expeter tamquam de re sua* " (cf. *Opusc.* 73 *de usuris*). Ratzinger expresses the sense of the later part of this passage again: "In the capital transaction the capitalist by no means turns over the property right to the business partners, but this remains with him. The merchant or businessman with whom he associates himself works with the risk of the capital lender."

[37]Cf. *Kölner Correspondenz*, published by Dr. P. Oberdörffer, 9th yr. vol. 1 and 2, p. 30.

[38]Cf. Schiffini I. c. p. 187ff. — Roman law provides four bases for occupation:

1. Gaius (I. 1, *Dig. de usurp. et usucap.*) says: "*Bono publico usucapio introducta est, ne scilicet quarumdam rerum diu et fere semper dominia incerta essent.*"

2. Neratius (*Dig. Pro suo*) : "*Usucapio rerum...propter ea, quae nostra existimantes possideremus, constituta est, ut aliquis litium finis esset.*"

3. *L. 7 Cod. De Praescript. 30 vel 40 annorum* indicates that the holder in good faith must be free from the *immortalis timor* of losing something of the good or the right which he holds.

4. Finally, Paulus says (I. 28 *Dig. De verborum significatione*): "*Vix est, ut non videatur alienare, qui patitur usucapi.* "

[39]The conditions which Roman law established are usually summed up in the verse: *Res habilis, titulus, fides, possessio, tempus.*

Chapter 8

OBLIGATIONS OF AND LIMITS ON PRIVATE PROPERTY

1. By private ownership a person appears to be entitled to have at his exclusive disposal a material good as something which belongs to him alone, and to use that to the exclusion of all other persons for his own advantage and in his own name. The owner is therefore empowered to dispose of the substance of the thing by processing, consumption, destruction, or sale. He has the right to use the object, to derive benefits from it and, as the prerequisite to all of this, to keep the thing in his own possession. Finally, by the full power which he has over the property, he can also transfer the power over, the possession of, the use of, and the derivation of benefits from the property, to another person by a contract.

That is how private property presents itself as the highest and most complete form of dominion over things which man enjoys.

Yet, that dominion over property is "the most complete" only in a relative sense, i.e., the most complete among the various forms by which every person can exercise dominion over a thing, but by no means simply an absolute, intrinsically unlimited and externally illimitable dominion that is without responsibility.

2. First of all, man must acknowledge that all creatures, and therefore all material goods, always remain essentially dependent on God, as creatures can belong fully and completely only to God. Accordingly, God emerges as the only really absolute owner of all things; and this right of God is inalienable because it is rooted in the essence of God and of creatures. No distribution, no possession, no law may and can change anything in this essential right of God, and in this essential subordination of the creatures.[1] In his relationship to God, man is and remains, as we said, always only the lien lord, the administrator, a user of his goods.[2]

But for that reason man also cannot wheel and deal with his goods as he pleases. His right to use affords him only the power to use the temporal goods according to God's will. Man must acknowledge the order which God established in the way things are used. He never has the right to take the use of the temporal goods away from the use for which God intended them. This first purpose of all temporal goods is, however, expressed as much in nature as in the words which God spoke to man after the creation: "See, I give you every seed-bearing plant over all the earth, and every tree that has seed-bearing fruit on it to be your food."[3] That, therefore, is the purpose of temporal goods: they are intended to serve for the preservation of the life of all who belong to the human species - to the human race.[4]

3. From this stem directly a series of moral and legal obligations with regard to the acquisition of material goods.

Above all, greed may never serve as the rule for the increase of possessions. St. Ambrose pillories with powerful blows this thieving vice:

> How far will your insatiable greed take you yet? Do you want to have the right to live alone on earth? It appears as though the poor person does you an injustice, because he still has his small possessions for which your avarice hankers. You appear to believe that what does not yet belong to you was taken from you unjustly. So that you will no longer have to see your neighbor owning anything, you want to extend your property to the ends of the earth!.... The earth was given to rich and poor alike. Why do you want to take possession of it all for yourself?[5]

If insatiable greed, taken by itself, is already a reprehensible vice, the order established by God is doubly violated by those unlawful means which avarice frequently avails itself of so as to increase riches: suppression of widows and orphans, exploitation of the poor and the weak, deception, usury, etc. "St. Ambrose called out to the usurers of his time:

> Since the goods of this earth are assigned to all, why do you take them away from the enjoyment intended for all? God gives us a superabundance; why do you bring us poverty? O how liable you are to punishment, who do not know any higher ambition but to see us stripped of everything; or who, in your quest for amassing wealth in your attics pretend to console yourselves that you can see in advance the coming lean years! And you call that cleverness, foresight, business genius? You ought to call that roguery, perfidy, heartlessness. No, you do not foresee evil in order to avert it; you speculate with our hunger in order to exploit it. Now what are we to call that? Is it commerce or theft? You are like robbers who spy the favorable moment in order to throw the passerby into the bush and strangle him! A curse on you usurers! You draw interest which cries to heaven from our misfortune, and you yourselves bring about crises in order to derive profit from them; your profit is the ruin of us all.[6]

4. As is the case with the acquisition of property, its use too is not left to the arbitrary discretion of the owner.

Above all, property ownership by no means provides the right to senseless waste. No one will be in a position to contest the kind of luxury which keeps itself within the limits of the station of life, which is nothing other than the more lavish use of good that one has according to reason and custom. However, that senseless luxury whereby goods are needlessly destroyed, appeals in vain to property ownership for its justification. For, property is justified precisely as a necessary means for mankind to achieve more efficient production, a more orderly use of goods, an improved provision for individuals, for the family, for the whole human race, but by no means as a means for vain and unreasonable and unwonted destruction of goods. That kind of luxury contradicts the destiny of goods, let alone the countless vices which get to be associated with it.

The property owner is morally obligated *to share with those in need from his overabundance.* He may not avoid this obligation of benevolence. [7] This is precisely what Leo XIII in the encyclical *Rerum Novarum* [8] impressed most sharply and with very special emphasis on the wealthy, when he warned at the same time that they should not pretend to be above the poor because of their riches, and that the poor too should not be inhibited because of their poverty:

> Therefore, those whom fortune favors are warned that freedom from sorrow and abundance or earthly riches are no guarantee of that beatitude that shall never end, but rather the contrary; that the rich should tremble at the threatenings of Jesus Christ — threatenings so strange in the mouth of our Lord; and that a most strict account must be given to the Supreme Judge for all that we possess.
> The chief and most excellent rule for the right use of money is one which the heathen philosophers indicated, but which the Church has traced out clearly and has not only made known to men's minds, but has impressed upon their lives. It rests on the principle that it is one thing to have a right to the possession of money, and another to have a right to use money as one pleases. Private ownership, as we have seen, is the natural right of man; and to exercise that right, especially as members of society is not only lawful but absolutely necessary. 'It is lawful,' says St. Thomas Aquinas,' for a man to hold private property, and it is also necessary for carrying on of human life.'[9] But if the question be asked, How must one's possessions be used, the Church replies without hesitation in the words of the same holy Doctor: 'Man should not consider his outward possessions as his own, but as common to all, so as to share them without difficulty when others are in need. Whence the Apostle saith, Command the rich of this world...to give with ease, to communicate.'[10] True, no one is commanded to distribute to others that which is required for his own necessities and those of his household; nor even to give away what is reasonably required to keep up becomingly his condition in life; 'for no one ought to live unbecomingly.'[11] But when necessity has been supplied, and one's position fairly considered, it is a duty to give to the indigent out of that which is over. 'That which remaineth give alms.'[12] It is a duty not of justice (except in extreme cases), but of Christian Charity[13] — a duty which is not enforced by human law. But the laws and judgment of men must give place to the laws and judgment of Christ, the true God; Who in many ways urges on His followers the practice of almsgiving — 'It is more blessed to give than

to receive;'[14] and Who will count a kindness done or refused to the poor as done or refused to Himself — 'As long as you did it to one of My least brethren, you did it to Me.'[15] — Thus to sum up what has been said: — Whoever has received from the Divine bounty a large share of blessings, whether they be external and corporal, or gifts of the mind, has received them for the purpose of using them for perfecting his own nature, and, at the same time that he may employ them, as the minister of God's Providence for the benefit of others. 'He that hath a talent,' says St. Gregory the Great, 'let him see that he hideth not; he that hath abundance, let him arouse himself to mercy and generosity; he that hath art and skill, let him do his best to share the use and utility thereof with his neighbor.'[16]

As for those who do not possess the gifts of fortune, they are taught by the Church that in God's sight poverty is no disgrace, and that there is nothing to be ashamed of in seeking one's bread by labor. This is strengthened by what we see in Christ Himself, 'Who whereas He was rich, for our sakes became poor;'[17] and Who, being the Son of God, and God Himself chose to seem and to be considered the son of a carpenter — nay, did not disdain to spend a great part of His life as a carpenter Himself. 'Is not this the carpenter, the Son of Mary?'[18] From the contemplation of this Divine example, it is easy to understand that the true dignity and excellence of man lies in his moral qualities, that is, in virtue; that virtue is the common inheritance of all, equally within the reach of high and low, rich and poor; and that virtue, and virtue alone, wherever found, will be followed by the rewards of everlasting happiness. Nay, God Himself seems to incline more to those who suffer evil; for Jesus Christ calls the poor blessed; He lovingly invites those in labor and grief to come to Him for solace; and he displays the tenderest charity to the lowly and oppressed. These reflections cannot fail to keep down the pride of those who are well off, and to cheer the spirit of the afflicted; to incline the former to generosity, and the latter to tranquil resignation. Thus, the separation which pride would make tends to disappear, nor will it be difficult to make rich and poor join hands in friendly concord.

But, if Christian precepts prevail, the two classes will not only be united in the bonds of friendship, but also those of brotherly love. For they will understand and feel that all men are children of the common father, that is, of God; that all have the same end, which is God Himself, Who alone can make either men or angels absolutely and perfectly happy; that all and each are redeemed by Jesus Christ, and raised to the dignity of children of God, and are thus united in brotherly ties both with each other and with Jesus Christ, 'the first born among many brethren;' that the blessings of nature and the gifts of grace belong in common to the whole human race, and that to all, except to those who are unworthy, is promised the inheritance of the kingdom of Heaven. 'If sons, heirs also; heirs indeed of God, and co-heirs of Christ.'[19]

5. *The property owner is a member of the political society;* and *property,* as the proofs of its justification indicate, is a social institution, insofar as it is not supposed to serve only the well-being of the individual and of the family, but must adapt itself to the welfare of the whole.

But it is with private property as it is with many other things. The institution itself, taken by itself is good. However, the abuse which human weakness or perversity chooses to inflict with it spoils everything and changes the blessing into a curse. Legitimate acquisitive interest turns into greed, and the exclusivity of property that is in the nature of the thing is all too easily turned into gruesome, heartless self-seeking. For every murder without exception, human hands are involved; they mix the poison, they lead to the dagger, they fire the revolver; no murder is conceivable without a human hand having been involved in it. Can we say therefore: the hands are the source of all murder? No, it is not the hand which is the source of the murder, but the fallen nature of man, his abandonment of God, which enables him to come on the idea of killing a fellow man, and to use his hand in order to accomplish that. The hand is a gift of God; but man can misuse it for murder. Likewise, private property is something that is provided by God, but man can abuse it.

It is precisely the possibility of abuse which imposes the obligation on the state to see to a structuring of private property that takes the rights of all into account.

Yet, what do we understand by a "structure of private ownership" and by a "good, healthy" ordering of private property?

In the broader sense, the expression " the ordering of property" designates at times the property situation within a political society, whether it is good or bad. The the shifting conditions and stages of social and economic life of a nation have the first decisive influence on the various structurings of property conditions; then there are the prevailing moral and legal views, and finally positive state legislation which is influenced by both of these factors.

In the narrower sense, an "order of private property" means the *sum total of those positive-legal provisions about the acquisition, the exercise, and the loss of property ownership within a political society.*

In the narrowest sense, finally, we understand by the "ordering of private property" that legal form and structure of property relationships within a political society by which the rights and obligations of individual property owners are kept in harmony with the rights and obligations of all. Thus, "order" is conceptually nothing other than the *proper* relationship between the parts and the whole, the means and the end.[20]

If we consider the concept of an order of private property in the broadest or even in the narrower sense, then we can distinguish between a good and a bad one, or a just and an unjust one.

An order of private property is "good" and at the same time "just" which presents itself as an effective application of the natural law principles about property and social life in keeping with historical circumstances.

If it does not take due account of the actual given conditions, the historical stage of development of social and economic life, if it stands in opposition to the divine moral laws and to natural individual and social rights, then it has no claim to being an effective good and just "ordering of private property," in the same sense as we speak of the "health" of a sick man. In truth it is a "disordering of private property" and as such it is the source of untold misery.

Specifically, an order of private property is "bad" which does not make it a point to prevent — to the extent that this is possible, that the human natural right to acquire property is made, either totally illusory for a part of the members of society, or that it is corrupted by human fault; and an ordering of property is *unjust* which advances even positively the private advantage of individuals at the expense of the whole community, the overall national welfare, — and it is objectionable if it is not in a position to protect property that has been acquired in an appropriate manner.

6. Therefore, the rightful admissibility of legislative restrictions on private property in general, cannot be doubted. Their establishment neither exceeds the power which comes with state authority, nor do they go against the essence and the purpose of the property right.

In order to present the admissibility of legal provisions about the acquisition and use of property, it is not necessary to resort to an unproven and unprovable "supreme dominion" (*dominium altum*) of the state over all objects of property.[21] The jurisdictional authority which state authority has in dealing with citizens of the state is enough for this purpose. For, if the right to acquire property is also provided to people by nature, then the actual acquisition traces back to the free exercise of human activity. This can, like everything which stems from liberty, take a form that varies greatly and can be good or bad, just or unjust. The same holds for the mode and method of using goods that come to be privately owned. But now it is necessary that this free activity which happens on the part of citizens of the state must be brought into harmony *with justice and with the general welfare of all of society*. That is why the property owner, as a citizen of the state, is subjected in many ways to the will of the lawgiver, but always only within those limits which are drawn by the purpose of the state.[22] St. Thomas Aquinas also teaches that. He requires that goods which are privately owned must all be made amenable to the general welfare "by proper laws and practices." That is how, according to him, the principle which he defends is fully realized, that so far as the care and administration of goods are concerned, this is left to the individuals, but the *use* should be of service to *all*.[23]

If this principle is duly observed, then the method of dealing with *immovable property* cannot be exactly the same as the treatment of movable property. Lehmkuhl says,[24]

> The opposite means denying the very difference between movable and immovable property, and its importance for all of social life. The legal treatment of a thing must correspond to the essence and the importance of the thing.

Taparelli stresses the same idea with even greater emphasis.[25] For, the land has a great economic and political importance for the whole nation; it is an indispensable basis of settlement, and for culture and higher civilization. Even if it is divided up, the land still remains the *common source of nutrition for the nation.*[26] National wealth, the strength of the state, its economic and political independence, are all essentially conditioned by healthy agricultural conditions.

7. The state, to be sure, has to safeguard civil liberty in establishing the order of property, and especially in determining the limits of property, so far as this is possible, and it must avoid any violation of *natural or acquired rights.* An attack by which duly acquired property robs the rightful owner, or which wholly abolishes any authority that is naturally associated with property, is not something to which the state has a right.

The *universal principle* according to which the activity of the state is regulated in this area was developed in a clear and convincing fashion by Taparelli.[27] Inasmuch as we presuppose that the owner may not abuse his power so as to harm the private rights of the individual fellow citizen, the question remains what sacrifice he must make in the interest of preserving and protecting the *public welfare* that is common to all. For this, Taparelli formulates the following law which ascertains the degree of his obligation to the whole without unjustly violating the individual owners' right to dispose of his property: *the measure of obligatory sacrifice by the individual for preserving the public welfare is determined according to the law of the conflict of rights.*

The citizen may undoubtedly maintain all of his powers to advance his true, i.e., ordered welfare, insofar as and so long as in the process he does not come into conflict with the rights of others. In the case of that *conflict,* the lower right must yield to the higher one. For, since both cannot apply at the same time, reason obviously requires the preference for the higher right; and it would be against healthy order if the lower right were to triumph at the expense of the higher one. But what is higher is: 1. the right which belongs to a higher and more general order. Therefore the right of the community takes priority over the right of the individual.

Secondly, a right which involves a greater, higher good, is also a higher right. And thirdly, there is the right which, *ceteris paribus,* can prove titles which are less dubious.

> Now we can easily see how useful it is for society if the principle of the conflict of rights is carefully applied in determining the public welfare; for, without such a principle, what is the public welfare? That which pleases each individual. If one wants to enjoy oneself, then the public welfare means public entertainment; if one wants to enrich oneself, then it means trade and commerce; if one wants to dominate, then it means war; and if one wants to rest, then it means peace, etc. In the name of the public welfare, we have seen in France terrorism erecting scaffolds and shedding innocent blood, just as in Jerusalem the Innocent was nailed to the Cross by the politics of Caiaphas — in the best interests of the people.[28]

Thus, it is not simply the preferences of those who happen to be in power, nor the fickle whims of a predominant majority which constitute the basis and the measure of legal restrictions on property ownership. Their justification lies in the clear natural law principle; and they find their limits where the universal natural law of reason gives rise in an objective, incontestable manner to the individual freedom of disposition. In other words, the limits lie where, and only where, free disposition would add up to an otherwise unresolvable conflict with the incontestable rights of the community, so that the right of individual freedom must yield to the higher right of the community. However, the essential right of the community, of political society, is the right which resides in the realization of its natural purpose, i.e., the right of the community of its members — to the extent that this is realizable — to safeguard, to preserve, and to fulfill the possibility that they, by acting freely, can accomplish and preserve their own private welfare. Where the accomplishment of this natural purpose of political society is placed in jeopardy, then the freedom of disposition on the part of the individual citizen must accept having limits placed on itself.

In order to accomplish the proper subordination of the individuals to the legitimate interests of the community, a direct incursion on property ownership is generally not called for.[29] As a rule it is sufficient if the state keeps the manner and form in which citizens make use of their property rights in harmony with the requirements of the general welfare. Thus, the state can spell out more specifically the natural law provisions with regard to the acquisition of private property, and determine in terms of what external prerequisites the natural law title to acquisition of property comes to apply.[30] — It can designate objects which should remain separate from individual private ownership. For, nature opposes only universal and exclusive collective ownership, but by no means the public property of the communities and of the state which is within the limits of what the common good calls for. — Of great importance for the general welfare, especially also for the prevention of an excessive concentration of ownership in the hands of a few is the development of the legislative right of contract. The law can establish the conditions under which a contract first attains full validity and liability, and it can also make provisions about the scope of the powers imparted by contracts; it can prohibit certain contracts of doubtful moral worth, or of a kind that are harmful to the community (stock market play), and it can subject them to penalties.

Also, it is within the state's power, insofar as clear requirements of the general welfare are involved, to establish provisions about the kind and manner of the use of objects of property. Thus, the state, in the event of a conflict with the public interests, can forbid the devastation of a forest, the turning of fields into forests and meadows on a broader scale, or leaving them fallow, etc. Also, we may concur with state authority if it prevents people from hoarding grain which is necessary to feed the nation, and to hold it in reserve solely for the sake of greater profit. We are entitled to use our property to our advantage, indeed in the most advantageous manner, but never for the ruin of others or of all, no matter how great the hoped-for advantage may be. This also resolves the question whether the state is authorized to put a limit on large stores in the interest of the middle class, and to tax progressively, etc.

If ecclesiastical and private charities are not sufficient to resolve the poverty and the misery of the poor, the state is also justified in imposing so-called poor taxes on the wealthy.[31]

Finally, very specifically, natural law principles require more detailed provisions about inheritance by positive state legislation. Here too, once again, the state can, without violating justice contribute very much by good laws to a healthy distribution of property, and to maintaining the general wealth of the nation. It will, on the one hand, divide up accumulated riches which people hold by fitting inheritance laws; and on the other hand, where it is historically justified and economically feasible, it may assure a continuance of family wealth by recognizing a moderate primogeniture law.[32]

In many nations, e.g., among the Israelites, and among the Germans during the Middle Ages, there was a legal custom to provide to the first born certain privileges with regard to inheritance. The French Revolution basically did away with the right of primogeniture. In any case the assumption for justifying that kind of arrangement was that proper care is assured for the education and support of the rest of the children. If this condition is fulfilled, then, under certain conditions there could be weighty reasons for the right of primogeniture, for the right of succession on an undivided farm, etc.[33] For, with equal division it is impossible to keep intact for the nobility or also for others established land-ownership — the kind of economic condition which provides the indispensable basis for its civil and political status. All advantages which stem from a certain stability among the ruling circles for the state and community would therefore disappear, quite aside from the fact that in some regions the most appropriate approach needed for working the soil could not apply if the estate were divided up. Even if it is true that the condition of the individual child who is born later may appear for the moment to be improved, the advantage is often worse in the long run than we may be led to believe upon superficial observation. First, with regard to the progeny overall. After three or four generations perhaps most of the family members may have fallen onto hard times. Also the individual child who is born later loses that significant security of being able to come back to the family in times of need and amid the manifold fortunes of life. Even if the daughters, in particular, are excluded from the inheritance where primogeniture prevails, they have a substitute to some extent in the wealth of their husbands, which in that system, in fact, experiences an increase. Furthermore, this inheritance averts a predominance of the financial aspect in concluding the marriage. The wife is sought after, cherished, and loved for her personal qualities. The marriage retains its high moral character, whereas today it is often degraded into a commercial venture.[34] The hostility toward all undivided estates, primogeniture, family estates, homesteads, etc. arises from individualistic liberalism which here once again poses as the angel of the light, and understands how to talk lovingly of the "natural honesty," and of the dangers of the concentration of ownership, etc. In fact, however, a primogeniture system that is properly formulated formally and materially establishes a secure barrier against the most frightful of all kinds of concentration, the capitalistic type which liberalism has brought us.

8. Just as the introduction of restrictions against arbitrariness in matters dealing with the acquisition and use of private property undoubtedly lies within the competence of the state and of state legislation, so, on the other hand, we cannot assert that such restrictions go against the nature and the system of the right of private property itself. The proof of that is already contained in what we have said earlier about the concept of private property, about the right to life which every man enjoys, about the establishment of private property on the basis of social perspectives. The moral character of the right of property, its essential relationship to the universal and higher right to existence, its equally essential connection, finally, to the requirements of life in society, — those are the factors which place the admissibility and necessity of limits on private property beyond any doubt.

Property of its nature provides power and control over a thing; moreover it gives rise to a social edge: it represents social power. Yet, despite all of that, we must not forget that it is not raw power, but a right, i.e., a moral entitlement, a potential — indeed a power, but not simply physical force, but a moral quality which therefore also can only command recognition so long as it remains on the solid ground of the moral order.

The materialistic world-view, at any rate, lacks the appreciation for this approach to property ownership. It still talks about a right, but that is merely a name. For it, right and might are identical. It knows no other right beyond "the right of the more powerful," that right which lasts only so long as it can compel its observance, but which disappears when a stronger person appears. Not so, reason.[35] It views a right as a moral one, i.e., an entitlement based on rational principles, not merely a physical capacity; and it regards this as inviolable, i.e., it presupposes in all other rational beings the moral obligation to recognize my own jurisdiction. The right, however, possesses that moral character and inviolability by its relationship to the will of God who alone can exercise the universally applicable, mandatory influence over all rational beings. In other words: the right is a right only because, and insofar as, it traces itself back to the order of the natural law as a component of the moral world order. Since God cannot contradict Himself, there is no law outside the moral law; i.e., independent of it or even in opposition to it: no law that goes against the legal order by which the relationships of people to one another are governed in social life according to the Divine plan.[36] Therefore it makes no sense to talk about an unconditional free, "absolute" property right. At the moment when property seeks to be "absolute," it stops being a right. It can only claim for itself the character and force of a right so long as it adapts itself to the universal moral order, in the natural and on the positive legal order that is based on it, by which the life of a community and the endeavors of mankind are regulated.

Among material rights, the *iura in re*, the right of private property, is the most perfect and highest, but by no means, as we have already indicated elsewhere, simply the highest right overall which man has with regard the world of things.[37] We may never forget that by the Divine ordinance, temporal goods are to serve not only the purposes of individuals, but the maintenance of the whole human race, the entire human species. Every individual person has, by virtue of that destiny, a personal right to acquire what he needs. With regard to what is material, this right is incomplete, because it does not provide any direct claim to a specific object. Only in the case of the most extreme need, that material imprecision and imperfection gives way, and we may take what is at hand without doing an injustice to the one who owned it until now. The right to life, to the necessary means to preserve life, thereby interposes itself as a higher right, before which the acquired property right has to recede. Every understanding authority will keep the abilities of property owners to acquire and dispose of property in harmony with the requirements of the general welfare of the nation, not only in order to conform to God's purposes which certainly did not make the world serve man so that it could save him from death by starvation only in the most dire need — and furthermore not merely to enforce the personal right to life which every citizen has, but also for the sake of the survival of society itself. The owners, however, will not be able to object to the assurance of the right to life for all citizens of the state, because the ultimate legal basis of his property must be sought precisely in the divine ordination of the world to serve the needs of all of humanity and the welfare of all of society.

This viewpoint too shows once again, if it is rightly understood, that limits imposed on property in the interest of the entire community and of the rights of others by no means contradict the nature and the essence of private property.

Property is not *an end in itself,* but only the means to see to the sustenance of mankind in a manner which conforms in a fitting manner to the welfare of the individual, the family, and the state. If property were "an end in itself," then it could not be restricted by any extrinsic concerns. But since it is merely a means to the end, it finds in its end the limits of its entitlement. According to its end, property is supposed to serve not only the arbitrary will of the owner, his enjoyment, and his fancy; but it is supposed to provide for him and his family in a manner conformable to the social order and the social well-being. All arguments which speak for the legitimacy and necessity of private property lead back to the designated purpose.

9. If there is talk here of "providing for" the individual and the families, we must warn against an exaggeration which emerges repeatedly. Does the necessity of the goods which are privately owned for the preservation of life establish also the positive limits to the legitimate acquisition of property? In other words: is "need" the positive measurement of the amount of property ownership that is allowed?

By no means, as anyone can easily see. For:

First, "need" is not suited to serving as a yardstick. "Need" is a concept with flexible limits. If I have in mind only the abstract nature of a person, then I can always assert that the needs of all people are equal, and that those involve food, housing, clothing. If I open my eyes to the real, concrete world, I will see immediately that needs turn out to be very different for different individuals according to age, sex, habit, health or sickness, the number of family members, etc. And that does not yet even take into account the powerful subjective, psychological factors for measuring "needs."

Second: the nature of the relationship to human ambition is in a position to provide far more goods than are necessary to satisfy only the most general needs.

Does not this obvious fact not show most clearly, that the limits of the property which I may own is in no way naturally established by the most general human needs?

Third: man also has a right to fulfillment. By his own resourcefulness he may improve the condition and the circumstances of himself and of those who belong to him. Indeed, it is precisely an advantage of human nature to provide for future needs, and to be able to provide an improvement of one's future condition. Is this natural advantage which elevates man above the animal, to be without any object and meaningless? Should the right to make use of his greater energy and resourcefulness to acquire more than others be thwarted?

Fourth: *Man has a natural right to the fruits of his labor.* For, with regard to my human nature, I am not obligated to serve someone else. I can provide my labor to others by a contract, in return for a just wage. But if I prescind from those kinds of accessory conditions, and if I consider only human nature, it is clear that what I do is entirely in my hands. For it is a part of me because it is an effect which proceeds from me. But the effect follows the cause, is contained in the cause, is a part of the cause. Now whoever wants to make a claim to what is rightly acquired by me, to the fruits of my exertion, he would rob me of what is mine without any right at all, as we indicated earlier in establishing the institution, private property. Now, however, because of the differing bodily, mental, moral capacities of the person, the working ability and performance of the individual persons will have to emerge as differing greatly for the individual person. One person works more and better than the other. Would it therefore not be a blatant injustice if we robbed the person who worked longer and with greater industry and skill, of his greater "work output," and kept his ownership at the level of "needs?"

Fifth: finally he who seeks to derive the positive limits for restricting the extent of the acquisition of ownership from universal human needs overlooks the fact that in the matter of ownership, it is not merely the needs of the individual and of his family, but also those of civil society which must be taken into account. However, this calls for differences in social standing and therefore also of ownership, on the basis of its organic character, and also because of cultural advancement. So people, according to their desire for fulfillment, expand and actualize human dominion over nature according to their energies and capacities; and finally, this happens also for the sake of the social order, so that citizens are allowed and legally protected in the rightful ownership of the differing results which they achieved quantitatively and qualitatively on the basis of their different talents or of specially favorable conditions. —

What has an entirely different meaning, however, is the question whether it is not the universal human need, but the social need which carries the implication of a negative limitation on the acquisition of goods. Incidentally, this question has been resolved in what was said above. For here we are no longer investigating the quantity of wants which a human being has as a person, in order to establish the proper measure of goods for him. It is far more a question of whether the goods available or attainable in a society may be taken possession of and administered by a portion of the citizenry at such a level and in such a way that the other portion can no longer satisfy its necessary, universal human needs. Obviously, that kind of situation will be the ruin of the state, and it will signify a grave violation of duty on the part of the public authorities. True, the state is not obligated of and by itself to provide food and work for its citizens. But it is really an essential part of its task to protect in an effective manner the right of all citizens to acquire their sustenance by work.

10. Where such principles find application, the free activity of property owners will be limited to not just a little, and their right of disposition will be restricted significantly. However, such limitation is necessary in the interests of justice and of the common good; it is not even actually an actual evil for the property; but it is actually good to the extent that the reduction of freedom in the individual order appears indispensable for participation in the goods of a higher *social order.* [38]

[1]Cf. S. Thomas, *S. Th.* 2, 2, q.66, 1: 1, 2, 106, 3c. — Lessius, *De perfectionibus moribusque divinis.* Edit. Roh (Freiburg 1861). *lib.* X, c. 3. — Wilh. Emm. v. Ketteler, *Die grossen Fragen der Gegenwart* (Mainz 1849) p. 6.

[2]Cf. Alfred Winterstein, *Die christliche Lehre vom Erdengut nach den Evangelien und apostolischen Schriften* (Mainz 1898) p. 15ff. 21f. 30ff. 45.

[3]Cf. *Genesis* 1:29. v. Ketteler, *op. cit.* p. 6,7.

[4]Cf. Gustav Ruhland, *Die Wirtschaftspolitik des Vaterunser* (Berlin 1895) p. 4f. — Franz Walter, *Das Eigenthum nach der Lehre des hl. Thomas* etc. (Freiburg 1895) p. 62ff.

[5]Cf. S. Ambrosius, *De Nabuthe* c. 1 & 3. — Cf. the excellent explanations by Dr. Georg Ratzinger, *Die Volkswirtschaft in ihren sittlichen Grundlagen* (2nd completely revised edition, Freiburg 1895) p. 43ff.

[6]Baunard, *Geschichte des hl. Ambrosius* (Freiburg 1873) p. 136.

[7]On the special tasks of Christian charity in the present, cf. the lecture by Prof. Dr. Franz M. Schindler in *Sociale Vorträge*, presented at the *Wiener sociale Vortragskurse* in 1894. Collected and published at the suggestion of the *Leo-Gesellschaft*, by Prof. Dr. F. M. Schindler (Vienna 1865) p. 119ff.

[8]Leo XIII, *Rerum Novarum*, paragraphs 18-21.

[9]2,2,q.66, a.2.

[10]2,2,q. 65,a.2.

[11]2,2,q.32,aa.6.

[12]Luke 11:41.

[13]St. Thomas (2,2,q.66, a.7) said: *Ea quae sunt iuris humani, non possunt derogare iuri naturali vel iuri divino. Secundum autem naturalem ordinem ex divina providentia institutum, res inferiores sunt ordinatae ad hoc, quod ex his subveniatur hominum necessitati: et ideo per rerum divisionem et appropriationem ex iure humano procedentem non impeditur, quin hominis necessitati sit subveniendum ex huiusmodi rebus. Et ideo res quas aliqui superabundantur habent, ex natuali iure debentur pauperum sustentatione.* The expression *naturali iure debentur* designates first of all, only a moral obligation, not exactly an obligation of *iustitia stricta,* the justice whose violation brings with it the obligation for restitution. The property owner should give of his superabundance. He, the owner, nevertheless has to take the initiative in such distribution. The distribution of the fruits furthermore remains a *dispensatio propriarum rerum,* of things which belong as much to the substance for the owner as the things themselves. Also the manner of distribution is left to the judgment of the property owner: Since there are many who suffer want, and since one cannot help all of them with the same things, the distribution of the things which belong to him is left to the judgment of each person, so that he may help those in need with those things." (S. Thom. I. 2). — There is only one case where the poor person himself may seize the initiative. That is the case of most dire need, when death and the danger of death threaten and there is no other resort — then, St. Thomas says, he is allowed to use the good of his neighbor even without his permission, to the extent that this is necessary to survive the actual condition of most extreme need. St. Thomas means that in such cases there can be no talk of theft or robbery. For, he recognizes the principle that "in the most dire need, everything is common," — obviously not in the sense of a positive community of goods, but only insofar as the property right of one person is not stronger than the right of the other to stay alive. As the one is entitled to use the good as its owner, so the other may appropriate it as a human being, because it is the only means for him to preserve his life. The *acquired* right of property must yield here to the *innate* right of self-preservation.

[14]Acts 20:35.

[15]Matt. 25:40.

[16]*In Evang. Hom.* IX, n.7.

[17]1 Cor. 8:9.

[18]Mark 6:3.

[19]Rom. 8:17.

[20]Cf. Baron v. Hertling, *Naturrecht und Socialpolitik* (Cologne 1893) p. 41ff.

[21]The "super-ownership" of the state or of society by no means exists in law; it is merely a fiction, and in addition, a dangerous fiction. We, for our part, do not see every kind of ownership as a "state benefice" or a "state stock," as Justus Möser expresses himself, or as others say, a "social benefice." Property is a fief of God; it is by no means a fief of society, and the owner is not a fief-holder of the state or of "society." The assignment of the human race as the owner of this earth does not confer on this race, and even less so on the "state' or on "society" actual positive common ownership; but it signifies, as we have already indicated previously, only an assignment of the earth to humanity in the generic sense (not in the collective sense), to negative common ownership. Each person who partakes of human nature should have and protect the right to acquire property from the world of goods. And for that reason, in order that this right will not become an illusion, state authorities have to see to it, to the extent that it is able, that it protects duly acquired property. For undoubtedly the person who strives by the use of his capacities to bring a portion of the world's goods under his control, and the one who already has a portion under his control stand at the same level so far as the community is concerned, insofar as both have the same claim to the effective protection of their rights whether they are innate or acquired rights. — It amounts to a scientifically untenable basis for limits on ownership when Treitschke says (*Der Socialismus und seine Gönner. Preuss. Jahrb.* 1882): "Property ownership comes into force only by recognition of it on the part of the state; and since the state confers the capacity by such recognition, so it also imposes obligations on the property owner, and it establishes limits according to its own will, which change constantly according to the needs of the community. No nation ever has seen property as such an uncircumscribed right as it appears to be in the theories of private law that is cut loose from public law."

[22]Cf. Schiffini, *Disputationes philosophiae moralis* II, 181ff.

[23]S. Thom. *Comment. in Aristot. Polit. lib.* II, *lect.* IV: "*Opportet enim possessiones simpliciter quidem esse proprias, quantum ad proprietatem dominii, sed secundum aliquem modum communes....Quomodo autem usus rerum propriarum possit fieri communis, hoc pertinet ad providentiam boni legislatoris.*" Many other passages from Thomas in Schaub, *Eigenthumslehre* p. 397ff.

[24]*Stimmen aus Maria-Laach* XLVIII, 285.

[25]*Op. cit.* I, 484.

[26]With reference to German law, Gerber says (*Zur Lehre vom deutschen Familienfideikommiss., Jahrb. von Jhering* I, 60): "The ownership of land in Germany never rated as a right with unlimited freedom; from the start it always involved an addition of moral or political obligations; it did not have simply the character of an exclusive right, but it was more like an *officium*. That is one of the most effective basic ideas of German law which was upheld throughout the whole course of its development, and which cannot be overlooked in the construction of present-day law." However, this concept of an *officium* must not be exaggerated in the sense as understood by state socialism, as if the land owner as such merely carries out an obligation which he got from the state. Yet the state may at any rate not be indifferent toward the distribution of land and the soil, and with regard to the way and manner it is worked. In terms of the economic and political point of view, much hinges on the fact that in the distribution of ownership the greatest possible part of the nation remains called to land ownership. But it is precisely from the distribution of land that the way land is worked depends to no small extent. In countries where large landed estates predominate, there is the danger of a less intensive cultivation, the suppression of grain-culture by pasture operation, of turning fertile acreage into hunting grounds and parks, etc. The most advantageous exploitation in the common interest of the resources in the soil is best observed where there is a strong, self-employed peasant class, where the large, mid-sized, and small holdings are found in a proper balance, without the excessive predominance of large landed estates, but also without excessive fragmentation. We will therefore have to approve wholeheartedly if the economic policy of the state, without any violation of rights — adopts such a situation as its goal, and strives effectively toward its realization or preservation. The exhaustive examination of the questions involved here must be left to the treatment of the agrarian question.

[27]*Op. cit.* I, 367.

[28]Taparelli, *op. cit.* I, 368ff.

[29]We are not talking here about the case of legally justifiable expropriation. For example if a state takes over for public purposes a parcel of land for the purpose of facilitating communication, the private party must yield. However he does have a right to full compensation for the value involved. It is only his ownership of that particular parcel of land which conflicts with the right of the community, not the value of the land as a part of his wealth. This value must therefore remain the possession of the previous owner. Taparelli, *op. cit.* I, 368.

[30]Cf. F. Hitze, *Schutz dem Handwerk* (Paderborn 1883) p. 39. "Ownership which is acquired once on the basis of the existing laws is sacred and inviolable; but the future pattern of ownership, the titles to acquiring ownership in the future, are naturally to be determined by legislation within the framework of the natural law."

[31]Cf. *Liberalismus, Socialismus und christliche Gesellschaftsordnung.* I. *Der christliche Staatsbegriff* (2nd ed.) p. 178ff.

[32]Cf. M. F. Le Play, *L'Organisation du travail* (Tours 1871) p. 499ff. 503ff. on the effect of inheritance law on the family.

[33]Cf. Schiffini I. c.p. 301ff.

[34]Cf. *Institut. de Droit Naturel par M. B. (de Lehen) tom. I, n. 303, quoted by Schiffini* I, c. p. 203.

[35]Cf. Theod. Meyer S. J. *Die Grundsätze der Sittlichkeit und des Rechts* (Freiburg 1868) p. 105. 113ff. 133.

[36]The moral "world order" establishes the relationships of people to God, to oneself, and to one's neighbor, and it constitutes the bonding material which God has placed around humanity for realizing and preserving social organization" (Theod. Meyer, *op., cit.* p. 117). Cf. Ferdinand Walter, *Naturrecht und Politik im Lichte der Gegenwart* § 60: "The basis for law and the concept, law, is the sense of right and conscience that is innate in man, which seeks the agreement of human actions and conditions with justice. In the process, we may not stand still, but must inquire into the objective factors which lie outside of the person on which justice itself rests. This objective, however, is the moral world order which transcends man; and the sense of right and the conscience are, in fact, the organs which God gave to man so that he can recognize this invisible order and get into contact with it. They are the eyes of the spirit which peer into the super-sensate world that is unreachable by the mundane eye. Thus, right and justice ultimately are the laws of the moral world order which flow from the qualities of God, which make themselves known as such by the organ of conscience, in other words, as the will of God and as a power which transcends the human beings."

[37]Cf. on this matter our explanations in *Liberalismus, socialismus und christliche Gesellschaftsordnung.* I. *Der christliche Staatsbegriff* (2nd ed.) p. 169ff.

[38]S. Thom. *De reg. princip.* I, c. 15: "*Sicut pars et totum quodammodo sunt idem, ita id, quod est totius, quodammodo est partis.*" *S. th.* 2,2,q.47, a. 10 *ad* 2: "Whoever seeks the common good of many, thereby seeks his own good for two reasons: 1. because one's own good cannot exist without the common good of the family, of the state, or of the empire. Therefore Valerius Maximus says of the ancient Romans: 'They preferred to be poor in a rich state, rather than rich in a poor state.' 2. Since the person is a part of the family or of the state, in considering his own private well-being, he must proceed from what is conducive to the well-being of society. We appraise the good condition of the parts according to their relationship to the whole, for Augustine says thus: 'It is disgraceful for each part, to not correspond to the whole.'" Cf. Schaub, *Eigenthumslehre* p. 393f. — Castelein, *Le Socialisme et le Droit de Propriété* (Brussels 1896) p. 234. 520ff. 530ff.

MELLEN STUDIES IN ECONOMICS